ST. JOSEPH'S COLLEGE OF EDUCATION LIBRARY

This book is issued in accordance with current College
Library Regulations.

DATE DUE AT LIBRARY LAST STAMPED BELOW

THE IMITATION OF CHRIST

THE IMITATION OF CHRIST

THOMAS À KEMPIS

TRANSLATED INTO MODERN
ENGLISH BY
EDGAR DAPLYN

SHEED AND WARD – LONDON

THIS EDITION FIRST PUBLISHED 1973
SHEED & WARD LTD.,
33 MAIDEN LANE,
LONDON WC2E 7LA

NIHIL OBSTAT : JOHN C. HOGAN, CENSOR
IMPRIMATUR : + RICHARD J. CUSHING, ARCHBISHOP OF BOSTON
BOSTON, 3 MARCH 1952

PRINTED IN GREAT BRITAIN BY
REDWOOD PRESS LIMITED
TROWBRIDGE, WILTSHIRE

"Nothing more holy, nothing more honourable, nothing more religious, nothing in fine more profitable for the Christian commonweal can you ever do than to make known these works of Thomas a Kempis."— Abbot Pirkhamer (1494)

CONTENTS

CONTENTS

BOOK II

THOUGHTS LEADING TO THE INWARD LIFE

BOOK III

OF INWARD CONSOLATION

BOOK IV

A DEVOUT CALL TO HOLY COMMUNION

TRANSLATOR'S PREFACE

THIS BOOK in its original language has a peculiar joy for those who can read Latin, but our translations load it with a ponderous style which makes the reading more of a duty than a pleasure. I have tried to avoid this tradition and hindrance by using as far as possible the living English of to-day.

The *Imitation of Christ,* or *Church Music* as some MSS. entitle it, was written by a Dutch monk who lived from 1379 to 1471. The popular opinion of his book, as known in our tongue, is that it only appeals to the strictly pious mind, and is not suitable for one living the ordinary work-a-day life. Such an individual taking up a copy of any English edition now in circulation would feel justified in his prejudice because he would find the language did not spring with natural freshness, but had the heavy touch of the pulpit and clerical library of other days.

À Kempis wrote so simply that one hardly recognises him in the long-winded archaisms of most of our editions. The mark of the Reformation period is seen in convictions that are set before an author's rights, by which words, sentences and even whole passages are altered or deleted. Controversialists deliberately cut out what they disapproved, or clouded the true significance with vague words. No mention must be made of the cross on a chasuble, or the high dignity ascribed to the priesthood, or the spiritual power of the words used in the act of celebrating, or the historic fact of the papacy, or the part they played in the book. This temper of mind so frankly unfair to À Kempis is embalmed in nearly all successive issues, and clothed in a laboured imitation of the Authorised Version of the Bible. Perhaps the Stanhope translation, which went through a vast number of editions, reaches the limit by its abundances of textual error, sectarian omissions and glosses, and the inclusion of long screeds of depressing comment. The bishop may almost be said to have hidden the original in a lawn surplice.

In the present translation the whole text is given as it still stands in the author's own handwriting, and any personal opinion of the translator has been repressed by keeping firmly in mind that the old monk wrote for the only body of Christians he knew, and also that no one has a right to mutilate for publication a signed work of literature. We should guard our classics both for their own qualities and for their historical value.

This book can be of practical help to anyone, whatever their faith may be, and is quite as effective now as when it was written. Its lucid sentences stir in us· the finest qualities, those we all too lightly ignore in the moulding of character, such as simplicity, fortitude, and the sense of awe. The book itself will open out its own treasures. It will stimulate that increasing modern sense of man's innate divinity, the call to spiritual knighthood by way of honour, frankness, love, self-control, honesty and conscience, reminding us of our own active part in aiming at the ultimate good for all. It opens the door of vision, awakens the imagination, compels us to think seriously of the implications of immortality, calls us to a Christ-like self-consecration to our race, reminds us of the emptiness of ambitions with their contempt for selfless ideals, yet stings us to become captains over our weaknesses, and in the so mechanical world of today would have us see the supreme worth of some kind of faith in God as the active good and the ultimate joy. These are sound helps to get out of one little book; they alone would have sealed its destiny to live, for they fling a glory over the morning's outlook, and when night falls they shine as guides to peace.

Millions have read this book. It is never out of print though it has no story to tell, even about Christ. Few know much about the writer who hid himself in the habit of a monk and let it be assumed that he was merely a patient copyist of pious works. Yet now and then he slipped in some book of his own for the monastery shelves. Hardly anyone knows of them. They are not easy to come by to-day. The rare student who hunts for a copy of the one complete edition, that of Sommalius in the seventeenth century, will require singular patience. But the *Imitation* itself has poured from a steady stream this four hundred and fifty years, surviving all the battles and changes of European faith, and keeping its hold equally on the Catholic south and the Protestant north. There can be little doubt that the new generation will find it though perhaps they will turn to it more readily if it speaks in the living tongue they use, as did that first translation of it, out of French, into the English of her own period, made by Margaret, mother of Henry VII.

The translation here offered is an attempt along that line, and the aim has been to present, with the freshness of a new work (so far as the text would permit), a book once written in a dead tongue, but still full of life; and to do this with such truth to the original that any reader unversed in Latin may feel he or she possesses the work as it was written, though not with the dryness of a crib.

Eliot Stock's facsimile of the manuscript completed by Thomas à Kempis in the year 1441, has been used side by side with Hirsch's careful text and notes. It has not been possible always to retain the terseness as well as the sensitiveness of the original; the rhythm and the frequent rhyme in the Latin have hardly been attempted here; but perhaps enough of the book's inspiring quality has been preserved to make new lovers of this profound yet simple work.

EDGAR DAPLYN.

BOOK I

REMINDERS USEFUL FOR THE SPIRITUAL LIFE

REMINDERS USEFUL FOR THE SPIRITUAL LIFE

1. Of the imitation of Christ, and indifference to all earthly vanities

HE THAT follows me is not walking in the dark, says the Lord. These are the words of Christ by which we are reminded how we should imitate his life and ways if we wish to be truly illuminated and freed from all blindness of heart. Therefore let it be our chief duty to meditate on the life of Jesus Christ.

Christ's teaching excels all the instructions of the saints, and he who has the spirit will find hidden manna there. But it so happens that many through frequent hearing of the Gospel feel little moved because they have not the spirit of Christ. He who would fully and with relish understand the words of Christ must strive to fashion his life wholly to his.

What good is it to you to argue profoundly about the Trinity if you lack humility and so displease the Trinity? Fine words indeed do not make one holy and righteous, but a virtuous life makes one dear to God. I would rather feel compunction than know its definition. If you knew the whole Bible by heart, and the sayings of all the philosophers, what would it all be worth without the love and grace of God? Vanity of vanities and utter emptiness, except to love God and to serve him only.

The highest wisdom is this:—to aim for the heavenly kingdom through indifference to the world. Vanity it is therefore to strive for perishable riches and to rely on them.

Vanity too it is to court honours and to set oneself out for lofty state. Vanity it is to go after fleshly desires and long for that by which you must presently be heavily punished. Vanity it is to wish for a long life and care little about a good life. Vanity it is to attend only to the life that is and not foresee the days that are ahead. Vanity it is to love what is passing at full speed and not hasten there where lasting joy awaits.

Frequently recall that saying:—the eye is not satisfied with the seen nor the ear filled with what is heard. Try then to draw your heart away from love of things visible and to bring yourself to the invisible. For by pursuing their sensual impulse men stain conscience and lose God's grace.

2. *Of thinking humbly about oneself*

ALL MEN naturally wish to have knowledge, but what does the knowledge convey without the fear of God. The lowly rustic who serves God may do better than the proud philosopher who neglecting himself reflects on the course of the heavens. He who understands himself well seems the poorer in his own eyes and finds no pleasure in the praises of men. If I knew everything in the world yet had not charity what would it help me before God who will judge me by the thing done?

Calm the excessive desire to know, for great distraction and delusion is found in that. The learned would gladly seem wise and be called so. Many things there are which when known do the soul little or no good. And most unwise is he who sets his mind on any other things than those which serve his well-being. Many words do not satisfy a soul, but a good life refreshes the mind, and a pure conscience warrants great confidence before God. The more and the better you know the harsher for that will you be judged unless you live the holier.

Do not allow yourself to be conceited about any art or science but rather dread the notoriety given you. If you think you know a great deal and understand sufficiently well, recognise at the same time that there are many more things which you do not know. Be not high-minded, but rather admit your ignorance. Why wish to put yourself up before others when you come upon many better educated and more steeped in reading. If you would know and learn anything to advantage, love to be unknown, and to be thought nothing of. The highest and most useful reading is this:—genuine knowledge of and looking down on oneself. To consider oneself nothing, and always to think well and highly of others, is great wisdom and perfection.

If you see another sin openly or do some grave wrong, you still should not think yourself the better: for you do not know how long you may be able to stand in goodness. We are all frail, but you should account yourself the frailest of all.

3. Of the teaching of truth

HAPPY THE one whom truth itself teaches, not by transient form and words but as self-revealed. Our opinion and our reasoning often fail us and seem so little. What use is great quibbling about hidden and unintelligible matters as to which we shall not be censured at the judgment because we were ignorant? It is a great folly that we reach out for the strange and harmful while ignoring the good and necessary. Having eyes we see not: and why should we trouble about *genus* and *species?*

He to whom the eternal Word speaks is delivered from a multitude of conjectures. All things spring from the one word, and all utter the one, and this is the beginning, which speaks also to us. No man understands or rightly decides without it. He to whom all things are one, and who brings all to the one, and sees all in the one, can be steadfast in heart and abide peacefully in God.

O God, the truth, make me one with thee in perpetual charity. It often wearies me to read and listen to many things: in thee is all that I will and desire. Be all the learned silent, all creation hushed in thy presence: speak thou alone to me.

The more a man is one with himself, and inwardly undivided, so much the more and deeper he understands without because he receives the light of pure understanding from above. A pure, simple and steadfast spirit is not dissipated among many activities, because all tasks are done for God's honour, and he endeavours to be at rest within himself from all self-seeking. What impedes and troubles you more than the unsubdued feeling of your heart? A good and devout man first sets out inwardly the things to be done. Nor do they draw him away to longings of a lawless inclination, but he himself bends them to the ruling of calm reason. Who has a harder fight than one who strives to master himself? And this should be our concern, that is: to conquer self, and daily become stronger, and to make for something better.

All perfection in this life has some imperfection knitted into it, and no speculation of ours is without its darkening mist. Lowly understanding of self is a surer road to God than a profound seeking after knowledge. Science is not to be condemned, nor the simple knowing of anything which is considered good in itself, and divinely ordered: but a good conscience and a virtuous life are to be put first. Because many struggle more to know than to live well, they often go astray for that reason, and bear little fruit or almost none.

O, if men applied as much effort to the uprooting of vices and the planting of virtues, as in stirring up controversies, there would not be such evils and scandals in the nation, nor so much laxity in religious communities. Surely on coming to the day of judgment we shall not be asked what we have read but what we have done: not how well we talked but how religiously we lived. Tell me, where are those lords and masters whom you knew well while they lived here and flourished in their scholarship? Now, others hold their prebends, and either do not know or never think of them. In their lives they seemed to be somewhat, but now there is silence about them. O how swiftly passes the glory of the world.

If only their lives had been one with their learning then had they studied and read right well. How many perish in a generation through fruitless knowledge, caring little about the service of God. And because they choose to be great rather than lowly they pass away with their thoughts. Truly great is he who has great charity. Truly great is he who in self is little and counts every pinnacle of honour as nothing. Truly wise is he who reckons all earthly things as refuse that he may gain Christ. And well and truly learned is he who does God's will and gives up his own will.

4. Of foresight in doings

ONE MUST not trust every word or impulse, but carefully and leisurely weigh the matter before God. Alas, evil is more readily believed and told about another than good, so weak are we. But men that are nearing perfection do not easily believe all that is said, because they understand human weakness, liable to evil, and frail enough in words.

It is very wise not to be headlong in deeds, nor to keep obstinately to one's own ideas. And along with this, not to trust every man's word, nor immediately pour into other's ears the things heard and credited. Keep company with a wise and conscientious man, and endeavour to be taught by one better than yourself, rather than follow your own discoveries. A good life makes a man divinely wise, and experienced in many ways. The lowlier he is in himself, and the more submissive to God, the wiser and more peaceful he will be in every way.

5. *Of reading holy writings*

TRUTH, NOT eloquence, is to be sought in holy writings. All sacred writing should be read in that spirit in which it was written. We must look for practical effect in the writings rather than for subtlety of word. We should read devout and simple books as willingly as the deep and profound. The authority of the writer should not trouble you whether he is of small or great scholarship: but let a love of pure truth attract you to the reading. Ask not who said this, but note what is said. Men pass away but the truth of the Lord remains forever. God speaks to us in various ways unmindful of the means.

Our inquisitiveness often holds us back in the reading of the scriptures when we want to understand and discuss just where it would be plainer to go on. If you would derive good, read humbly, honestly and loyally, without ever wishing to have a name for learning. Question freely and silently, listen to the words of the saintly not letting the stories of those of old displease you, for they were not told without a purpose.

6. *Of uncontrolled feelings*

WHENEVER A man has an unruly longing for anything he is at once restless within himself. The proud and the covetous never rest: the poor and lowly of spirit are kept in abounding peace.

A man who is not yet completely dead to self is soon tempted and overcome by petty and worthless things. Weak in spirit, and still in a measure carnal and inclined to sense perceptions, he can hardly drag himself away from earthly longings. And so he is often dejected when he does withdraw himself, and is easily angered if anyone opposes him. But if he follows out what he craved for he is soon depressed by the accusing voice of conscience because he followed up his passion which in no way helps towards the peace for which he looked.

In resisting the passions then, but not in being enslaved to them, the heart's true peace is found. For there is no peace in the heart of a carnal man, nor in a man given up to outward things, but in one who is fervent and spiritual.

7. *Of avoiding vain hope and elation*

VAIN IS he who puts his trust in men or in created things. Let it be no shame to you to serve others for love of Christ, and be looked upon as poor in this world. Do what is in you to do, and God will strengthen your good will. Rely not upon your knowledge, nor the cleverness of any living being: but rather on the favour of God, who assists the lowly and brings down those who think much of themselves.

Do not glory in riches if they come, nor in friends because they are powerful, but in God who gives all, and beyond all longs to give himself. Do not pride yourself on fineness or beauty of body which may be spoiled or marred by a touch of sickness. Do not be pleased with yourself on account of ability or genius, lest you displease God from whom comes the whole of whatever native good you possess. Do not reckon yourself better than others, lest you be held inferior in the eyes of God who knows what there is in a man. Be not conceited over good works, for God's judgments are unlike those of men: often that which pleases men displeases him. If you have some good quality believe better things of others, so that you may preserve humility. It does not hurt to place yourself below all, but it is most harmful to set yourself before even one. Perennial peace is with the lowly, but in the heart of the proud is envy and constant chafing.

B

8. Of guarding against excessive familiarity

Do NOT open your heart to everyone, but put your case before the wise and God-fearing. Seldom be with the young and with strange people. Use no flattery with the rich, and do not push yourself eagerly among the great. Mix with the lowly and simple, the devout and obedient, and talk of things which build one up. Be not intimate with any woman, but in general commend all good women to God.

Choose to be intimate with God and his angels only. Kindness is to be preserved towards all, but intimacy is not safe. It sometimes happens that a person unknown is radiant with goodly fame yet his actual presence dims the brilliance for the eyes of those who see him. Sometimes we expect to please others by mixing with them, and instead we displease them through some fault of character seen in us.

9. Of obedience and subjection

IT IS a very great thing to persevere in obedience, to live under a prelate, and not to be a law to oneself. It is much safer to stand in subjection than in command. Many are more under obedience from compulsion than from affection, and they easily feel hurt and complain. Yet they cannot win mental freedom unless they submit themselves whole-heartedly for God's sake. Run here or there, you will not find rest except in humble subjection under the prelate's rule. The dream of position and change has deceived many.

True it is that everyone readily makes for his own liking, and is mainly inclined to those who agree with him. But if God is in our midst we must sometimes give up our own feeling, for the sake of peaceful good. Who is so wise that he can fully understand everything?

Therefore do not be too settled in your own opinion, but cheerfully be willing to listen to the ideas of others. If your

idea is good, but you give it up for God, and follow anoth
you may gain the more for that. For I have often heard th.
it is safer to hear and accept advice than to give it. It ma
also come about that each one's thought may be good, but
to refuse to agree with others when reason or the case itself
demands it, is a sign of pride and obstinacy.

10. *Of guarding against unnecessary talk*

AVOID THE throng of men as much as you can, for the talking
about worldly things is very entangling, even when carried
on with quite simple intention. For we are soon tinged with
vanity and led captive. I often wish I had kept silent, and
had not been among men.

But why do we talk and gossip together so freely when we
seldom revert to silence without an attack of conscience?
The reason we talk so readily is that by conversing together
we expect to get comfort from each other, and hope to
relieve a heart wearied with distracting thoughts. And we
talk and think most freely about those things we best love
or wish for, or those we feel to be against us. But alas,
often emptily and without result. For this outward relief is
in no slight way a weakening of inner and divine well-being.

So one must watch and pray lest time pass idly away. If
it is allowable and useful to speak, talk of what will edify.
Bad habit and carelessness of our own good makes for the
unsealing of our lips. But a faithful comparing together of
spiritual matters helps no little on the soul's way: most of
all where those of like mind and spirit meet together in
God.

11. *Of gaining peace and ardour while pressing on*

WE COULD have more peace if we would not busy ourselves
with the sayings and doings of others which are not our
affair. How can he remain long at peace who mixes himself

up with the concerns of others, who searches for outside interests, who little or seldom concentrates himself within? Blessed are the single-minded for they shall have much peace. Why were some of the saints so perfect and contemplative? Because they strove to deaden themselves in every way to all earthly desires, and so to cleave to God from the marrow of the heart, and were freely at leisure for themselves. We are too engrossed with our own passions, and too anxious about transitory things. For we rarely overcome one vice completely, and do not burn for daily progress: therefore we remain cold and lukewarm.

If we were thoroughly dead to self, and less confused within, then we might taste divine things, and experience something of celestial contemplation. The whole impediment and the greatest is that we are not freed from passions and earthly longings, nor do we try to tread the perfect way of saints. Then when the least adversity comes, we are too swiftly cast down, and turn to things human for relief.

If we could strive to stand to the fight like brave men we should see the Lord's help descending upon us from heaven. For he who gives us times to fight that we may conquer is himself ready to aid those who, fighting, trust in his grace. If we base advance in religion so much on outward observances our devoutness will soon be at an end. But let us lay the axe to the root that, purged of passions, we may come to possess a mind at peace. If every year we uprooted a single vice we should soon become perfect men.

But on the contrary we often feel now that we were better and purer at the beginning of our conversion than after many years of profession. Ardour and progress should increase daily: but now it is looked on as a great thing if one can retain a part of the early fervour. If we used a little force at the beginning then afterwards we should be able to do everything with ease and joy. It is hard to put aside habit, but it is harder to go against one's own wish.

Yet if you do not conquer things small and light how will you overcome the more difficult ones? Resist your inclination at the start, and unlearn the bad habit, lest perhaps little by little it lead you into greater trouble. O if you could see what peace to yourself and joy to others you could bring by holding yourself well in hand, I think you would be more anxious for spiritual growth.

12. Of the use of adversity

IT IS good for us at times to have some burdens and adversities, for they often call a man back to his heart, that he may recognise himself to be in exile, and not fix his hope on anything earthly. It is good for us sometimes to endure contradictions, and to be thought of as bad or imperfect, even when we do and mean well. Such things often help towards meekness, and protect us from idle boasting. For then we look to God, the better inward witness, when we are disparaged from without by men, and no good is credited to us. Therefore a man should so fortify himself in God that he does not need to seek after many human consolations.

When a well-intentioned man is troubled, or tempted, or afflicted by evil thoughts, then he understands his greater need for God without whom he realises he can do no good thing. Then too he is sad, he laments and prays because of the unhappiness he suffers. It is then he is tired of living any longer, and wishes death would come, that he might be released and be with Christ. Then once more he truly perceives that complete security from care, and fulness of peace, cannot exist on earth.

13. Of resisting temptations

As LONG as we live on earth we cannot be without trial and temptation. Whence it is written in Job: a man's life on earth is temptation. Everyone should therefore be solicitous about his temptations, and watch with prayers lest the devil find an opportunity to entrap him: for he never sleeps, but goes about seeking whom he may devour. None is so perfect and holy that he has not temptations sometime: we cannot live entirely without them.

Yet temptations are often very good for us, though they may be troublous and burdensome: for through them a man is humbled, cleansed and taught. All the saints passed through many troubles and temptations, and still went on. And those who could not endure the tests were rejected and left.

There is no order so holy, nor place so secluded, where there are no temptations or adversities. There is no man quite secure against temptations as long as he lives, for it is from within ourselves that we are tempted, since we are born in passionate desires. One temptation or trial going, another comes: and we shall always have something to bear with, for we have lost the blessedness of our original felicity.

Many endeavour to escape from temptations and fall the deeper into them. We cannot conquer by mere flight, but by patience and true meekness we become stronger than all foes. He who only avoids the outer side, and does not pluck up the roots, will make little way. In fact, temptations will return swifter to him, and he will feel them worse. Little by little, and by patience together with calmness, you will overcome by God's help better than by your own rigour and persistence. Get advice more often in temptation, and refuse to deal harshly with the tempted, but pour in comfort, as you would wish done to you. The beginning of all evil temptations is unsteadiness of mind, and faint trust in God; for as a ship without a rudder is driven here and there by the waves, so a man, careless and drifting in his purpose is assailed in various ways.

Fire proves iron: and temptation the upright man. We often do not know what we are able to do, but trial shows what we are. One must be vigilant, especially at the beginning of temptation; for then the foe is more easily beaten if, checked from entering the door of the mind, he be met at the threshold when he first knocks. Hence someone said: Resist beginnings; remedy comes too late. For, first there comes to mind a simple thought, then a strong mental image: after that a sense of pleasure, then a perverse impulse, and assent. And thus gradually the malignant foe enters fully, since he was not resisted at first. And the longer one is careless about resisting, so much the weaker is he every day, and the foe more powerful against him.

Some suffer greater temptations at the start of their conversion, but others towards the end. Some actually suffer badly throughout their whole life. Others are tempted lightly enough according to the wisdom and fairness of divine ordering which weighs the standing and merits of men, and foreordains everything for the well-being of his chosen. Therefore we should not despair when tempted, but beg God more fervently that he will stoop to help us in every trial: he who surely, according to Paul's saying, will provide with the temptation a way out so that we can bear up under it. Let us humble our souls then under God's hand in every temptation and trouble, for he will save and uplift the lowly in spirit.

By temptations and tribulations a man is tested as to what progress he has made, and in that his reward stands greater, and virtue shines more clearly. It is no great thing for a man to be devout and fervent when he feels no burden: but there can be hope of great progress if he carries himself patiently in a time of adversity. Some are protected from great temptations yet are often overcome in little things every day, in order that they who are feeble in such small trials, being brought low, may never rely on themselves in great ones.

14. Of avoiding hasty judgment

TURN YOUR eyes on yourself, and beware of judging the actions of others. In judging others a man troubles himself to no purpose, is frequently mistaken, and easily does a wrong: but in judging and analysing himself he always labours fruitfully.

As we feel towards a matter so we often judge of it, thus easily losing a sound decision through a personal liking. If God were always the pure aim of our desire we should not be so easily irritated by a resistance to our opinion. But there is often something lurking within, or even coming from the outside, which alike draws us with it. Many aim overtly at their own ends in the things they do, and are unaware. They seem to be quite peaceful when things happen as they wish and think. But if it should prove other than they desire they are at once disturbed and sad.

Through differences of thought and opinion dissensions often enough arise between friends and fellow-citizens, between the religious and the devout. Old habit is hard to give up, and no one is easily led beyond his own point of view. If you lean more on your reason and activity than on the subjective power of Jesus Christ, seldom or tardily will you become enlightened: for God wants us to be perfectly submissive to him, and borne beyond all reasoning by a burning love.

15. Of work done for love

FOR NOTHING in the world and for the pleasing of no man is any bad thing to be done: but yet for the service of the needy a good task must sometimes be put aside, or at least exchanged for a better. For in doing this the good deed is not lost, but changed into a better.

Without love, external work produces nothing, but whatever is done for love, however small and contemptible, becomes wholly fruitful. For God considers more the purpose with which you work than the actual work done. He does much who loves much. He does much who does a thing well. He does well who serves the community rather than his own choice.

That often seems to be charity which is more of the physical self, because natural inclination, self-will, hope of reward, and love of gain will rarely be wanting. He who has true and perfect charity seeks self in nothing, but only desires God's glory to be wrought in every way. So too he envies none, for he loves no special delight of his own, nor wishes to find joy in himself, but chooses to be made blessed in God above every good. He ascribes nothing good to any man, but traces it entirely to God, from whom, fountain like, all things flow: in whom all the saints rest at last. O, he who has a spark of true charity should surely feel all earthly things to be utterly void.

16. Of bearing with others' failings

WHAT A man cannot better in himself or others, he must patiently bear with till God wills otherwise. Think of it as being perhaps thus for your probation and patience, without which our deserts do not weigh much. Amid such burdens you should pray that God may stoop to help you, and that you may bear them with a good heart.

If someone who is spoken to once or twice will not give in, refuse to contend with him, but leave it all to God who knows well how to change evil into good in order that his will and honour may be wrought in all his servants.

Try to be patient in bearing with others' failings and all kinds of weaknesses, for you too have many which must be put up with by others. If you cannot mould yourself exactly as you would, how can you get another to be satisfying to you? We would readily have others perfect and yet not amend our own defects. We want others rigidly corrected and are unwilling to be corrected ourselves.

B*

The wide freedom of others displeases us, and yet we would not be denied whatever we ask. We wish others to be bound by rules, and will ourselves in no way be held in. So plain it is, how rarely we weigh our neighbour as ourselves.

If all were perfect what should we then have to endure from others for God? But now God has so arranged that we may learn to bear each other's burdens, for none is faultless, none without a burden, none sufficient to himself, none wise enough in himself: but we must bear with each other, comfort each other, help, teach, and advise each other. For the strength that each has will best be seen in the hour of adversity. Because such hours do not make a man weak, but show what kind of man he is.

17. *Of the monastic life*

You MUST learn to break in self in many ways if you wish to keep in peace and concord with others. It is no light thing to live in a monastery or in congregation and remain there without complaining, and continue faithful even unto death. Blessed is he who has lived there well and finished happily. If you would hold out as you should and press on, think of yourself as an exile and pilgrim on earth. You must become a fool for Christ if you want to lead a religious life. Habit and tonsure contribute little: but change of character, and entire killing out of the passions, make the true religious.

He who seeks anything but the purely Divine and the welfare of his own soul, will find nothing but trouble and sorrow. Nor can he stand long as a peace-maker if he does not try to be less than and subject to all. You have come to serve, not to rule: know that you are called to endurance and work, not to ease and idle talk. Here then men are tried as gold in the furnace. Here none can settle unless he determines to abase himself whole-heartedly for God.

18. Of the examples of the holy fathers

LOOK INTO the vivid examples of the holy fathers, in whom shone true perfection and religion, and you will see how little it is, indeed almost nothing, that we do. Ah, what is our life if compared with theirs? Saints and friends of Christ, they served the Lord in hunger and thirst, in cold and bareness, in labour and fatigue, in vigils and fasts, in prayers and holy meditations, in many persecutions and taunts.

O how many and grave the troubles they suffered, the apostles, martyrs, confessors, virgins, and all the others who resolved to follow the footsteps of Christ. For they cared not for their souls in this world if only they might possess them in the life eternal.

O how strict and renounced a life the holy fathers led in the desert; what long and heavy temptations they came through; how often they were distressed by the enemy; what frequent and fervent prayers they offered up to God; what rigorous abstinences they practised; what great zeal and ardour they had for the spiritual way; what vigorous war they waged in extirpating vices; what a pure and straight mind they kept towards God. They toiled by day, and at night were free for long spells of prayer, though during work they by no means ceased from mental prayer. They spent their whole time profitably: every hour seemed short for devoting to God; and in the great sweetness of contemplation they were even drawn to forget the need of bodily food. They put aside all riches, dignities, honours, friends and kinsmen; they wished to retain nothing worldly; they scarcely partook of the necessaries of life; they even regretted serving their bodies in things needful.

So they were poor in earthly things, but very rich in grace and virtues, outwardly destitute but inwardly refreshed with divine grace and comfort. To the world they were strangers, but to God close and familiar friends. To themselves they seemed as nothing, and to this world a scorn: but in the eyes of God they were precious and beloved. They were grounded in true humility, lived in simple obedience, walked in love and patience, and so grew daily in spirit, and won deep grace with God. They are given as example for all the religious; and should challenge us more to go on well than a host of languid ones who enfeeble.

O how great was the fervour of all religious in the beginning of their holy training. O what devotion of prayer, what rivalry of virtue, what thorough discipline, what reverence and obedience under the master's ruling flourished in all. The traces left still testify that they indeed were holy and perfect men who fighting so actively trod the world under foot.

In these days we think highly of one who does not actually break the rule, or who patiently puts up with what he has agreed to. O the indifference and carelessness of our outlook, that we so quickly fall away from our first fervour and through lassitude and lukewarmness are already tired of the life. I would that the gaining of virtues may not wholly sleep in you who have often seen many examples of devoted ones.

19. Of the training of a good religious

THE LIFE of a good religious should be refined with every virtue so that inwardly he may be what he outwardly seems to men. And really he should be inwardly much more than is seen from without, for our overseer is God, whom we ought to revere exceedingly wherever we are, and walk pure as angels in his sight. Each day we should renew our intention, and quicken ourselves to fervour, as though today we first entered on the changed life, and say: Help me Lord God in good intention and in thy holy service, and let me now begin today perfectly, for what I have so far done is nothing.

As our intention is, so is the course of our advance, and there must be steady application for one who would make good progress. If he who resolutely plans often fails, what of him who seldom or with little determination plans anything. Yet the giving up of our purpose happens in many ways, and a slight omission of exercises rarely passes without some loss. The intention of the upright depends more on the grace of God than on their own wisdom, and they always rely on him for whatever they take up. For man proposes, but God disposes, and a man's road is not within himself.

If for the sake of duty or brotherly service some wonted exercise is at times omitted it may easily be regained afterwards. But if through mental tedium or negligence it is lightly let slip, it is a real fault and will be found harmful. Strive as we may we shall easily fail in many ways. Yet some fixed plan must always be laid down, and especially against those things which most impede us.

Our outward and inward affairs must alike be looked into and set in order because both bring us on the way. If you cannot concentrate continually, do so at all events sometimes, and at least once a day, namely, in the morning or at night. In the morning make your plan; at night run through your conduct, what you were today in word, deed, and thought; for in these perhaps you often displeased God and your neighbour. Gird yourself like a man against devilish villainies: bridle appetite, and you will more easily restrain every inclination of the flesh. Never be quite idle, but either be reading, or writing, or praying, or meditating, or working in some way for the common good.

Yet bodily occupations are to be undertaken with discretion, and not taken up in the same way by all. Matters which are not public concerns should not be openly displayed, for private things are more safely dealt with in seclusion. But take care lest you be slack about the common good, and keener for private ends; but once you have fully and properly fulfilled what you ought to do and are charged with, then, if you still have free time, give yourself to what your own devotion desires. All cannot have one training, but one is better for this, another for that.

So too, for certain times different exercises seem suitable, some for holy-days, others more fitting for week-days. Some we need in time of temptation, and others in time of peace and quiet. Some we love to dwell on when sad, and others when we are happy in the Lord. During great festivals good exercises are to be renewed, and the prayers of saints to be more fervently implored. From feast to feast we should prepare as if about to leave this world and come to an eternal festival. Therefore we should carefully prepare ourselves at holy seasons, and live more devoutly, and keep every observance more strictly, as if shortly to receive the reward of our labour from God. And if it be delayed let us account ourselves the less well prepared and still unworthy of such glory as shall be revealed to us at the appointed time, and let us strive the better to make ourselves ready for the end. "Blessed is the servant," says Luke the evangelist, "whom the Lord when he comes shall find on guard. In truth I say to you he will set him over all his goods."

20. Of love of solitude and silence

SEEK A fit time to be at leisure with yourself, and meditate often upon the good gifts of God. Put aside mere inquisitiveness; read deeply such subjects as rather touch the heart than keep the mind busy. If you will withdraw yourself from needless talk and idle wandering, and not listen for news and rumours, you will find fit and sufficient time to pursue good meditations.

The greatest saints shunned human company when they could, and chose to serve God in solitude. Someone has said: "As often as I went among men, I returned less of a man." This we often feel when we have gossiped a long time. It is easier to be quite silent than not to say a word too much. It is easier to hide at home than to be sufficiently watchful abroad. Therefore he who intends to attain the inward and spiritual must withdraw himself with Jesus from the crowd.

No one goes about with safety but he who would gladly stay hidden. No one safely speaks but he who would willingly keep silent. No one is safely set above who would not cheerfully be subject. No one safely gives orders but he who has thoroughly learned to obey. No one can safely be glad unless he has in himself the witness of a good conscience.

Yet the security of saints sprang always from fear of God; nor were they less careful and humble in themselves because they shone with great qualities and grace. But the assurance of the depraved arises from pride and presumption, and turns at last to self-delusion. Never promise yourself security in this life, however good a monk or devout a hermit you seem. Often those highest in men's esteem have been seriously endangered by their own excessive confidence. So it is better for many that they should not be altogether free from temptations, but often attacked, lest they be too sure, or perhaps uplifted in pride, or else too freely turn to outward comforts.

O if a man never sought for fleeting joy, nor ever engrossed himself with the world, what a good conscience he might retain. O if he could cut away every useless care, and think only of things wholesome and divine, and build all his hope on God; what great peace and rest he would have. No one deserves heavenly comfort unless he has diligently trained himself in penitent consecration.

If you would feel this to the very heart, enter your cell, and shut out the noise of the world, as it is written: in your resting places you shall feel deeply. In the cell you find what you often miss outside. The cell constantly used becomes sweet; ill-attended it begets dislike. If in the beginning of your turning to God you have stayed in it and kept it well, it will afterwards be to you a beloved friend and a most pleasing relief.

In silence and stillness a devout soul goes on and learns the secrets of the scriptures; there it finds streams of tears in which it may wash and purify itself each night, that so much the closer it may be to its maker, as the further it is from all earthly unrest. God with holy angels comes close to him who withdraws himself from acquaintances and friends.

It is better to hide away and take care of one's true self, than to make one's mark but neglect self. It is praiseworthy for a religious man to go seldom abroad, to avoid being noted, even to be unwilling to see men. Why wish to see what one may not have? The world passes away and the longing for it. Sensual longings draw us astray, yet when the hour is gone, what do we carry back but a laden conscience and a divided heart? A merry outing often brings a sorry return: and a night of high spirits makes the morning sad. So every carnal joy comes on smiling but at last bites and kills.

What can you see in other places that you cannot see here? Look at the sky, and earth, and all the elements, for from these all things are made. What can you see anywhere under the sun that can last long? You expect perhaps to satisfy yourself, but you can never reach that. If you could behold everything at this moment what were it but an empty dream? Lift your eyes to God on high, and pray for your wrongdoings and omissions. Leave vanities to the vain: aim you only at those things which God directs. Shut your door behind you, and call Jesus your beloved to you. Stay with him in your cell, for you will not find such peace elsewhere.

If you had not gone outside, nor listened to any hearsay, you would have remained in true peace; it is because the hearing of new things sometimes delights you that you afterwards have to endure the heart's restlessness.

21. Of heartfelt penitence

IF YOU would make any progress, keep yourself in the fear of God, and refuse to be too free, but repress all your feelings by discipline, not yielding yourself to foolish pleasure. Give yourself up to quickening of heart and you will soon attain a devout spirit. The prick of conscience opens up many good things which laxity has a way of quickly losing. It is wonderful that a man can ever be perfectly happy in this life if he ponders and reflects on his exile and the many perils of his soul. Through lightness of heart and indifference to our failings, we do not feel the sorrows of our soul; but often laugh emptily when rightly we should weep. There is no true freedom nor real joy except in fear of God through a pure conscience. Happy the man who can throw off the load of distraction, and concentrate himself on the one aim of holy penitence. Happy is he who puts from him whatever can stain or burden his conscience.

Resist manfully; habit is overcome by habit. If you know how to let men go their ways, they will cheerfully leave you to do your own work. Do not be drawn into other people's affairs nor involve yourself with the concerns of your superiors. Always keep an eye on yourself first, and especially be mindful about yourself before all those you love. If you do not get men's goodwill, refuse to be sad about that; but let this grieve you, that you do not carry yourself so well and watchfully as it becomes God's servant and a devout religious to live.

It is often more of a gain and safer for a man not to have many comforts in this life, especially those of the flesh. Yet we are at fault if we do not have divine ones, or rarely feel them; for then we do not seek for the heart's awakening, nor do we cast hollow and outward comforts entirely aside. Acknowledge yourself unworthy of divine comfort, but deserving increased tribulation. When a man becomes perfectly contrite then for him the whole world is a burden and a bitterness.

A good man finds cause enough for sorrowing and lamenting. For whether he takes note of himself or thinks of his neighbour, he knows that none here lives without trouble. And the more sternly he examines himself, so much the more he grieves. The grounds of true sorrow and inward penitence are our sins and vices in which we lie so bound that we can hardly look up to heavenly things.

If you thought more often of your death than of length of life, you would without a doubt correct yourself more earnestly. If too you would weigh in your heart the future pains of hell or purgatory, sure I am you would willingly bear any labour and sorrow, and would dread no austerity. But because these thoughts do not penetrate to the heart, and we still love allurements, therefore we remain cold and extremely lax. Often it is poverty of spirit at which the unhappy body so easily complains. Pray therefore humbly to the Lord that he may give you a spirit of repentance, and say with the prophet: "Feed me Lord with the bread of tears, and give me a measure of tears for drink."

22. Of the thought of human unhappiness

WHEREVER YOU are, and wherever you turn, you are unhappy unless you turn yourself to God. Why are you vexed because a thing does not succeed as you would wish? Who is there who has everything he wants? Not I, nor you, nor any man on earth. There is no one in the world without some trouble or tight place even though he be king or pope. Who is it has the better part? The one who can endure anything for God.

Many fools and weaklings say: see what a good time that man has, how rich, how great, how powerful and mighty. But set your mind on heavenly riches, and you will see that all these temporal goods are nothing, but very uncertain, and, even more, burdensome, because they are never held without anxiety and fear. A man's happiness is not in possessing wordly things in abundance; just a little would suffice for that.

To live on earth is actually a kind of unhappiness. The more a man wishes to be spiritual the more bitter the present life seems to him; because he feels more intensely, and sees more clearly, the failures through human corruptness. For to eat, drink, watch, sleep, rest, labour, and submit to the other needs of nature, is really a great trial and affliction to the devout man who would gladly be relieved and free from every failing. For the inner man is deeply depressed by bodily necessities in this world.

Whence a prophet prays devoutly that he may be freed from them as far as possible, saying: "Lift me out of my necessities, O Lord." But woe to those not knowing their poor state, and greater woe to those who love this pitiable and perishing life. For some cling so tightly to it that although they can hardly by labour and begging get necessaries yet if they could but live here for ever they would care nothing for God's kingdom. O mad are they, and faithless in heart, these who have fallen so deeply earthward that they can relish nothing but the fleshly. But yet these unfortunates shall at last feel how paltry and worthless was that which they loved.

On the other hand the saints of God and all the devout friends of Christ considered not what pleased the flesh nor what bore fruit in this life, but their whole hope and intent panted for everlasting posessions. All their longing was uplifted towards the enduring and invisible, lest by love of things seen it should be drawn down to the lowest depths. Brother, resolve not to lose confidence in pressing on towards the spiritual life; you have yet time and the hour. Why will you put off your decision? Rise and begin at once and say: now is the time to act; now is the time for fighting; now is the fit time to amend.

When you are sick and troubled then is the time to win through. You must go through fire and water before you reach the place of refreshing. Unless you deal firmly with sin you will not overcome it. So long as we bear this frail body we cannot be sinless, nor live without fatigue and pain. Eagerly would we be at rest from all trouble; but because we lost innocence by sin, we also let true blessedness go. Therefore you must have patience, and await God's mercy, till this adversity is over and death is swallowed up by life.

O how great is human frailty which is ever inclined to bad ways. Today you confess your sins, and tomorrow do again what you confessed. At the moment you determine to keep guard, and an hour later you act as if you had never made the decision. Rightly therefore should we humble ourselves, nor ever think any great thing of ourselves, since we are so frail and changeable.

Besides, that which with much effort we hardly gained even by grace, can speedily be lost by carelessness. What will happen in the end to us who so early grow lukewarm? Woe to us if we thus settle down to rest, as if peace and safety were already accomplished, when no sign of true holiness has so far appeared in our daily ways. It is important that like good novices we should yet again be taught the best methods if only in the hope of some future amendment and greater spiritual progress.

23. Of meditating on death

It will very soon be over with you here; reflect how it will be with you elsewhere. Today man is; and tomorrow he has vanished. But when he is taken out of sight he also soon passes out of mind. O the dullness and hardness of the human heart, that only dwells on the present, and does not look forward more to the future. You should so master yourself in every act and thought as if you were about to die this very day. If you had a clear conscience you would not be much afraid of death. It would be better to beware of sins than to fly from death. If you are not ready today, how will you be tomorrow? Tomorrow is an uncertain day; how do you know you will have a tomorrow?

What good is a long life when we amend so little? Ah, long life does not always improve us, but often adds rather to wrong-doing. If only we could spend one day well in this world! Many count the years of conversion yet often the fruit of amendment is small. If it is fearsome to die, perhaps to live on will be more dangerous. Blessed is he who always keeps the hour of his death in sight, and daily holds himself ready to die. If you have ever seen any man die remember how you too will go the same road. When it is morning reflect that you may not reach evening. But when evening is done, do not promise yourself a morning. Be ever ready then, and so live that death may never find you unprepared. Many die suddenly and unexpectedly, for in the unlooked-for hour the Son of Man will come. When that last hour shall arrive you will begin to think differently about your whole past life, and be exceedingly sorry you were so careless and slack.

How happy and sensible is he who strives now to be in life what he would choose to be found in death. For perfect disdain of the world, fervent longing to advance in virtues, love of discipline, labour of penitence, quick obedience, denial of self, and bearing with any adversity whatever for love of Christ, will give great assurance of dying happily. You can do a great deal of good while you are in health, but I do not know what you can do when sick. Few are made better by sickness itself; just as many who make pilgrimages are seldom made the more holy.

Do not rely on friends and relatives, nor put off to the future your soul's welfare; for men will forget you sooner than you think. It is better to make timely provision now, and to set forward some good, than to rely on help from others. If you are not solicitous for yourself now, who will be anxious on your behalf in the future? Now is the most precious hour; now are the days of safety; now the acceptable time. But how sad that you do not spend this better when you could buy with it that by which you could live for ever. The time may come when you will long for one day or hour for making good; and I do not know whether you will get it.

Ah dearest, from what a great peril you can free yourself, and from what great fear be delivered, if only you will be apprehensive and regardful of death. Endeavour so to live now, that in the hour of death you may be able to rejoice rather than fear. Learn now to die to the world, that then you may begin to live with Christ. Learn now to be indifferent to all things, that then you may press on freely to Christ. Chasten your body now by hardship that you may then have sure confidence.

Ah fool, why think of living long when you have no certainty of a day? How many are mistaken and unexpectedly snatched away from the body. How often you have heard men say, he is killed by the sword, he is drowned, he broke his neck falling from a height, he choked while eating, he met his end while at play; one perished by fire, another from plague, another by a robber; and so death is the end of all; and man's life passes suddenly like a shadow.

Who will remember you after death; and who will pray for you? Do, do now, beloved, whatever you can do; since you know not when you will die, nor do you know what will follow for you after death. While you have time, gather undying riches for yourself. Think of nothing but your eternal welfare; care only for the things of God. Make friends now for yourself by honouring the saints of God and imitating their conduct; so that when you fail in this life, they may receive you into the eternal abodes. Keep yourself as a pilgrim and stranger on earth to whom the affairs of the world seem nothing. Keep the heart free and uplifted to God, for here you have no abiding city. Thither daily direct your prayers and sighs, that after death your spirit may be worthy to pass happily to the Lord. Amen.

24. Of judgment and the penalties of wrong-doers

IN ALL matters look to the end, and how you will stand before the strict judge to whom nothing is hidden; who is not won over by gifts and accepts no excuses, but will judge as is right. O pitiable and foolish sinner, what answer will you give to God who knows all your wrong-doings; you who dread at times the glance of an angry man? Why do you not prepare yourself for the day of judgment, when none will be able to make excuse or defence for another, but the burden of each will be enough for himself alone?

At this moment your activity is fruitful, tears acceptable, sighs heard, the grief that satisfies and purifies. Great and wholesome purgation has the man who, bearing injuries, grieves more for another's evil thoughts than for his own injuries; who cheerfully prays for those crossing him, and heartily forgives offences, who is not backward in begging forgiveness from others, who is moved to pity more easily than to anger, who often does violence to his very self, and strives to subdue the flesh entirely to the spirit. It is better to purge sins and cut away vices now than to keep them to be purged in the future.

Truly we delude ourselves by the inordinate love we have for the flesh. What else will that fire devour but your sins? The more cautious you are now for your own self, and go after the flesh, the harder will you pay for it later, and store greater material for the burning.

In whatever ways a man has sinned, in those will he be the heavier punished. There shall the malingerers be driven with burning goads, and the gluttonous be tormented with prodigious hunger and thirst. There the lovers of luxury and pleasure shall be drenched in burning pitch and stinking brimstone; and like mad dogs the envious shall howl in their anguish. There will be no sin that will not have its own peculiar torment. There shall the proud be filled with every confusion, and the miserly be pinched with wretched poverty. There a single hour will be more laden with pain than a hundred years of hard penance here. No rest is there nor solace for the reprobate; while here one does sometimes rest from toil and enjoy the comfort of friends. Be anxious and pained about your sins now so that in the day of judgment you may be secure among the blest. For "the righteous will stand with great steadfastness against those who straitened and kept them down"

Then will he stand to judge who now submits himself humbly to the judgments of men. Then will the poor and lowly have abounding confidence, and the proud shrink at terror from every side. Then will he be seen to have been wise in this world who learned to be a fool and a scorn for Christ. Then will every trial patiently borne be pleasing, and "all iniquity shall shut its mouth". Then will every devout spirit rejoice, and all the non-religious mourn. Then will the harassed body be more delighted than if it had always been fed on delicious things. Then will the mean garb shine, and the fine-woven robe be heavy with gloom. Then will the poor little house be more praised than the gilded palace. Then will steadfast patience avail more than all the world's might. Then will simple obedience stand higher than all earthly cleverness. Then will a pure and good conscience more gladden a man than learned philosophy. Then will contempt of wealth weigh more than all the worldling's treasure. Then will you have more comfort from devout prayer than from delicate fare. Then will you rejoice more at having preserved silence than for long-drawn gossip. Then will holy actions be worth more than many beautiful words. Then will austere life and arduous penance be more pleasing than every earthly amusement.

Teach yourself to suffer in small things now, that then you may be given freedom from heavier pains. Test here first what you can bear hereafter. If now you can endure so little, how will you be able to sustain unending torments? If a little suffering makes you so impatient now, what will gehenna do then? Look, frankly you cannot have two joys: to taste delights here in the world, and afterwards to reign with Christ. If right up to this very day you had always lived in honours and pleasures what would it all profit you if you happened to die now, at this instant?

So all is vanity except to love God and serve him only. For he who loves God wholeheartedly, fears neither death, nor punishment; neither judgment nor hell; for perfect love gives sure access to God. But he who still likes to sin, it is no wonder if he fears death and judgment. It is at least a good thing that though love may not yet recall you from sin, still, the fear of gehenna may force you. But he who puts the fear of God behind him, will not last long in goodness but will the quicker fall into the snares of the devil.

25. Of fervently amending the whole of our life

BE VIGILANT and active in God's service and often think over the life to which you have come, and why you gave up the world. Was it not that you might live for God, and become a man of spiritual life? Be fervent then in going onward, for you will shortly receive the reward of your efforts; and then there will be no more fear or sorrow within your borders. You will toil a little now and find a great rest, indeed perpetual happiness. If you continue faithful and zealous in your doings, God will undoubtedly be faithful and generous in rewarding. You must keep a good hope that you will win the palm, but not be too confident lest you become sluggish or conceited.

When a certain anxious soul, wavering oft between fear and hope, and worn out with distress, once threw himself down in prayer before the altar in church, he turned these things over within himself, saying: "O if I could but know that I should still persevere," and immediately heard within the divine answer: "What if you knew this, what would you do? Do now what you would do then, and you will be quite safe." And soon, consoled and strengthened, he gave himself up to the divine will, and the anxious restlessness ceased. And no longer would he inquisitively seek to know what there might be for him in the future; but set himself the more to learn what God's satisfying and perfect will might be for the beginning and completing of every good work. "Hope in the Lord, and do good," says the prophet, "and dwelling on earth thou shalt feed on his rich store."

There is one thing that deters many from going on and fervently improving: dread of the difficulty, or the effort of the fight. They certainly advance most beyond others in virtues who strive manfully to overcome the things that are most trying and contrary to their own desire. For a man makes most way, and gains fuller grace where he most conquers self that it may die into the spiritual. But all men have not as much to overcome and deaden. Yet one striving diligently to excel will make more progress, even though he has many more passionate feelings than another who is more level-minded but less keen for virtues.

Two things especially help towards great improvement: namely, to withdraw oneself by force from that to which nature is viciously inclined, and to pursue zealously that good which we most need. Also try more to avoid and overcome those things which most frequently displease you in others. Make your headway in every direction, so that, if you see or hear of good examples, you are fired to imitate them. But if you consider anything blameworthy, take care that you do not the same; or if at any time you have done so, quickly try to correct yourself. As your eye observes others, so you too are noted by them.

How sweet and joyous it is to see fervent and devout brothers working together and well disciplined. How sad and depressing it is to see the disorderly goings-on of those who do not follow up that to which they were called. How harmful it is to leave the purpose of one's vocation and turn our thought to what is not our commission.

Keep your settled purpose in mind, and set before you the image of the crucified. You may well be ashamed in looking into the life of Jesus Christ, that you have not yet tried more to model yourself on him, though you have been a long time on God's road. The religious who trains himself intently and devoutly in the most holy life and passion of the Lord, will find there abundantly everything useful and necessary for him, nor need he look beyond Jesus for any better thing. O if the Jesus of the cross could enter into our heart, how quickly and sufficiently we should be taught.

A fervent religious takes and bears in good spirit all things that are laid on him. The careless and lukewarm religious has trouble on trouble, and feels restriction on every side because he lacks inward support, and is prohibited from seeking it outside himself. A religious who lives without discipline is open to grave disaster. He who looks for laxity and ease will always feel restraints, for one thing or another will displease him.

How do so many other religious manage, who are bound tightly enough under cloistral discipline? Seldom going outside, they live apart, eat poorest food, are coarsely clad, labour much, speak little, watch long, rise early, prolong prayers, read copiously, and keep ward over self by every discipline. Look at Carthusians, Cistercians, and monks and nuns of various religious orders, how they rise every night to sing psalms to the Lord. And therefore it should be a disgrace for you to be indolent in so holy a work when such a host of religious begin to praise God.

Oh if we had nothing else to do but to praise the Lord with all the heart and mouth. Oh if you never needed to eat or drink or sleep, but could praise God for ever, and could be entirely free for spiritual endeavours; then you would be far happier than now when enslaved to the body by every kind of necessity. Would there were not these necessities, but only the spiritual foods of the soul which alas we too seldom taste.

Whenever a man arrives at this, that he looks for his comfort from no created thing, then first God begins to be perfectly known by him; then too will he be quite content with whatever happens. He will then be neither exultant about a great thing nor gloomy about a small, but leave himself utterly and trustfully to God, who is all in all to him, to whom nothing ever perishes or dies, for to him all are alive, and serve instantly at a beck.

Always keep the end in mind, and that time lost never returns. Without care and steady application you will never acquire the virtues. If you begin to grow cool you begin to do badly. But if you give yourself with fervour you will find great peace, and feel the effort lighter through God's grace and the love of virtue. An ardent and attentive man is ready for everything. There is more work in resisting vices and passions than in sweating with physical tasks. He who does not try to shun small faults slips by little and little into greater ones. You will always be glad at evening if you have spent the day fruitfully. Watch over yourself, rouse yourself, prompt yourself; and whatever others may do, never neglect yourself. You will advance in proportion to the force you bring to bear upon yourself. Amen.

BOOK II

THOUGHTS LEADING TO THE INWARD LIFE

THOUGHTS LEADING TO THE INWARD LIFE

1. Of the Inner Life

"THE KINGDOM of God is within you," says the Lord. Turn yourself whole-heartedly to the Lord, and let this sad world go, and your soul will find rest. Learn to make light of the outward, and to yield yourself to interior things, and you will see the kingdom of God coming within you. For the kingdom of God is a peace and joy in the holy spirit which is not given to the irreligious. Christ will come to you, showing you his comfort, if you prepare a worthy dwelling-place for him within. All his glory and beauty is from within, and there he finds his delight. Frequent is his coming to the inner man, sweet the converse, gracious the comfort, much the peace, most wonderful the friendship.

Come then faithful soul, prepare your heart for this spouse that he may deign to come to you and dwell in you. For thus he speaks: "If anyone loves me, he will keep my word, and I will come to him, and make a home with him." Give place to Christ then, and deny an entry to all others. When you have Christ you are rich and satisfied. He himself will be your prudent and faithful steward in every way, so that you need not rely on men. For men soon change and quickly fall away, but Christ remains for ever and stands by firmly to the end. Great reliance is not to be placed on a frail and mortal man, even if he be helpful and cared for, nor much dejection felt if at times he turn and speak against us. Those who are with you today may to-morrow be against, and in veering round often change like the wind.

Put all your trust in God, and let him be your veneration and your love. He will decide for you and do well whatever is best. Here you have no lasting city, and wherever you may be you are a stranger and a pilgrim, nor will you ever have rest unless you are inwardly one with Christ. Why gaze around here when this cannot be the place of your rest? Your dwelling should be in the heavenly, and all earthly things should be regarded as a passing show. All pass away, and you alike with them. See that you do not cling, lest you be held and perish.

Let your meditation be with the Most High, and your prayer directed ceaselessly to Christ. If you know not how to explore the high and heavenly, take rest in the passion of Christ, and dwell freely on his sacred wounds. For if you go devoutly for help to the wounds and precious marks of Jesus, you will feel great comfort in trouble, and not heed much the gibes of men, and will bear disparagements lightly. Christ on earth was also scorned by men, and in greatest need was abandoned to insults by acquaintances and friends. Christ chose to suffer and be despised, and dare you complain of anything? Christ had adversaries and detractors, and would you have everyone friends and benefactors? Whence will your patience be crowned if it meets no antipathy? If you want to endure no opposition, how will you be a friend of Christ? Hold out with Christ, and for Christ, if you would reign with Christ.

If once you could perfectly enter the inner life of Jesus, and taste a little of his ardent love, then you would care nothing about your own gain or loss, but would all the more rejoice in bearing insult, because love of Jesus makes a man indifferent to himself. The lover of Jesus and of truth, one of real inner life and released from unruly emotions, can cheerfully turn himself to God, and rise beyond himself in spirit, and in enjoyment rest.

He who understands all things as they are, not as they are said or reckoned to be, is wise indeed, and taught more by God than by men. He who knows from within how to go, and expects little from outward things, neither needs places, nor looks for times for keeping devout exercises. An inward man quickly pulls himself together, because he never lets himself go entirely after externals. Outward toil does not obstruct him, nor business necessary at the time, but as things come so he adapts himself to them. He that is thoroughly ordered and methodical within does not trouble about the strange and perverse doings of men. A man is impeded and distraught in proportion to the interests he attracts to himself.

If all were right with you, and you were pure throughout, everything would turn to good for you and help you on. But as it is, many things annoy and often puzzle you, simply because you are not yet perfectly dead to self, nor set apart from all earthliness. Nothing so stains and grips a man's heart as an impure love of created things. If you put away external comfort you can peer into heavenly things and be constantly joyous within.

2. *Of humble submission*

THINK NOT much about who will be for you or against you, but be careful and act so that God may be with you in everything you do. Keep a clear conscience and God will surely protect you. For whom God chooses to help the spite of none can hurt. If you know how to suffer and be silent you will undoubtedly see the help of the Lord. He knows the time and the way of delivering you, and so you should yield yourself to him. It is for God to help, and to set free from every stress.

It is often very helpful towards preserving a deeper humility, that others know and disapprove of our faults. When a man humbles himself on account of his failings, then he easily conciliates others, and gently gives satisfaction to those angry with him. God protects and delivers the humble; he brings himself down to the humble man; he bestows great favour on the humble one, and after his humiliation uplifts him to glory. He unveils his secrets to the humble, and sweetly calls and draws him to himself. The humble, whilst suffering distress, is filled with peace, for he stands with God and not with the world. Consider yourself not to have made any progress unless you feel yourself inferior to all men.

3. Of a good peacemaker

KEEP YOURSELF at peace first, and then you will be able to make others peaceful. A peace-making man does more good than one very learned. A passionate man turns even good to bad, and easily thinks evil. A good peacemaker turns everything to good. He who truly lives in peace is suspicious of none. But he who is discontented and excited is tormented with various mistrusts; he is neither at rest himself, nor allows others to be at rest. He often says what he ought not to say, and says nothing of what it were much better for him to do. He looks carefully at what others are bound to do, and ignores what binds himself.

Therefore first keep zealous guard over yourself, and then you will be rightly zealous for your neighbour. You know well enough how to excuse and colour your own doings, but you are not willing to accept excuses from others. It would be more just to accuse yourself and to excuse your brother. If you would be borne with, bear also with the other.

See, how far you are still from true charity and humility, which knows not how to be angry or indignant with any but self only. There is nothing great in mingling with the good and mild, for this naturally pleases us all; and everyone gladly enjoys peace, and likes those most who agree with him. But to be able to live peaceably with the harsh and perverse, or with the disorderly, or with those who cross us, is a great gift, and most laudable, and manfully done.

There are some who maintain themselves in peace, and keep peace with others too. And there are some who neither possess peace themselves, nor leave others in peace; they are harmful to others, but always more harmful to themselves. And there are some who keep themselves in peace, and endeavour to bring others back to peace. Yet all our peace in this sorry life lies more in lowly endurance than in not feeling adversities. He who knows best how to suffer will retain the greater peace. Victor of himself is he and master of the world, Christ's friend and heaven's heir.

4. *Of a pure mind and simple intention*

BY TWO wings a man is uplifted from things earthly, by simplicity and purity. Simplicity should be in intention, purity in affection. Simplicity reaches out for God, purity apprehends and tastes.

No good activity will hinder you if you are inwardly free from disordered love. If you strive and seek for nothing else but God's pleasure and a neighbour's good you will fully enjoy inward freedom. If your heart were right then every creature would be a mirror of life and a volume of holy teaching. There is no creature so small and mean that it does not reflect God's goodness. If you were inwardly good and pure then you would see and thoroughly understand all things without difficulty. The pure heart penetrates heaven and hell.

As anyone is inwardly so he judges outwardly. If there is a joy in the world surely the man of pure heart has it. And if there is anywhere trouble and stress, the evil conscience knows this best. As iron thrust into the fire loses its rust and is completely brought to white heat, so a man turning himself wholly to God is stripped of apathy

C

and transformed into a new man. When a man begins to grow cool, then he shrinks from a little exertion, and readily accepts external comfort. But when he begins to master self perfectly and to walk on God's road, then he deems those things light which earlier he felt were heavy for him.

5. Of thinking about oneself

WE CANNOT trust over much in ourselves because grace is often lacking in us, and understanding. The light within us is small, and we soon lose this by want of care. Often too we do not notice how inwardly blind we are. We frequently do wrong, and make it worse by excuse. At times we are stirred by passion and think it zeal. Slight things in others we condemn, and pass over our own greater ones. We feel quickly enough and harp on what we undergo from others, but do not notice what others suffer from us. He who well and straightly weighs his own doings is not likely to judge anything about another harshly.

The inward man sets the care of himself before all cares; and he who turns his attention diligently to himself is easily silent about others. You will never be inward and devout unless you keep silence about others, and keep an eye specially on your own self. If you are utterly intent on God and yourself, what you see outside will move you but little. Where are you when you are not present to yourself? And when you run through everything what have you gained if neglecting yourself? If you would have peace and true oneness you must put all else aside, and keep only yourself before your eyes. You will accordingly gain much if you keep yourself at leisure from all temporal cares. You will certainly fail if you count on anything temporal.

To you let nothing be great, nor high, nor pleasing, nor acceptable, unless it be purely God or God's. Reckon as totally void whatever comfort comes from any created thing. The soul that loves God looks down on everything less than God. God, the alone, eternal, and measureless, filling all; the soul's relief, the heart's true joy.

6. *Of the happiness of a good conscience*

THE PRIDE of a good man is the witness of a good conscience. Keep a clear conscience and you will always have happiness. A good conscience can bear a great deal and is really happy amid adversities. A bad conscience is always timid and restless. You may rest sweetly if your heart does not reproach you. Refuse to rejoice except when you have done well.

The wicked never have true joy, nor feel inward peace, because there is no peace for the wicked, says the Lord. And if they should say "We are at peace, evils will not come upon us, and who will dare to hurt us?", do not believe them; for the anger of God will suddenly rise, and their deeds be brought to naught, and their plans melt away.

To glory in tribulation is not hard for one who loves: for so to glory is to glory in the Master's cross. Brief the glory which is given and received of men. Sadness ever haunts the glory of the world.

The pride of the good is in their consciences, and not in the mouth of men. The joy of the upright is from God, and in God, and their gladness springs from truth. He who longs for true and eternal glory has no wish for the temporal. And he who looks for temporal renown, and does not despise it from his soul, is clearly shown to love the heavenly less. He has large tranquillity of heart who heeds neither praises nor censures. He whose conscience is clean will easily be content and at peace. You are not the holier if praised nor the baser if blamed.

What you are, that you are: nor can you be called greater than you are before God. If you keep your mind on what you may become in your inner self, you will not care what men may say about you. Man looks at the face, but God into the heart. Man thinks of things done, God assuredly weighs intentions. Always to do well, and to think little of oneself is a mark of the lowly soul.

To refuse to be consoled by any created thing is a sign of great purity and inward confidence. He who requires no outside evidence in his favour shows that he has given himself up entirely to God. "For not he that commends himself," says blessed Paul, "is approved, but he whom God commends." To walk closely with God, and not be controlled by any feeling from without, is the grounding of the inward man.

7. *Of the love of Jesus beyond all*

BLESSED IS he who realises what it can be to love Jesus, and to think nothing of himself compared with Jesus. He must leave the thing prized for the one beloved, since Jesus wishes to be loved alone beyond everything. Love of the created is deceptive and fickle: love of Jesus is faithful and steadfast. He who clings to the creature, falls with its falling: he that embraces Jesus grows stronger through all time.

Love him and retain him as friend who, when all things fade, will not leave you nor let you go to the end. From all else you must be parted, whether you will or no. Keep near to Jesus, living or dying, and entrust yourself to his safe keeping who, when all fail, alone can help you. Your beloved is of such a nature that he will not allow a rival, but alone will have your heart, and sit like a king on his own throne. If you could thoroughly free yourself from every creature, Jesus would gladly stay with you.

Whatever you have found in men, as separate from Jesus, you will discover to be almost total loss. Neither trust nor lean on the wind-blown reed: for all flesh is grass, and like the flower of grass all its glory will be shed. You will quickly be deceived if you have such regard for the outward appearance of men. For if you expect your own satisfaction and gain from others, you will often have a sense of loss. If you seek Jesus in everything, Jesus you will surely find. But if you seek self, self you will certainly find, but to your ruin. For if a man does not seek after Jesus, he does himself more harm than could the whole world and all his enemies.

8. *Of the intimate friendship of Jesus*

WHEN JESUS is present all is well and nothing seems difficult. When Jesus is absent all is hard. When Jesus does not speak within, comfort is worthless. Yet if Jesus speaks but a single word, great comfort is felt. Did not Mary Magdalen rise at once from the place in which she was weeping when Martha said to her, ''The Master is here and calls you''? Happy hour when Jesus calls the spirit from tears to gladness. How dry and hard you are without Jesus: how foolish and empty if you desire anything apart from Jesus. Is not this a greater loss than if you should lose the whole world? What can the world offer you without Jesus? To be without Jesus is a bitter underworld: and to be with Jesus, a sweet paradise. If Jesus were with you no foe could harm. He who finds Jesus finds good treasure, even a good beyond every good. And he who loses Jesus loses much indeed, even more than the whole world. Most poor is he who lives without Jesus, and most rich is he who stands well with Jesus.

It is a fine art to know how to live with Jesus, and a great wisdom to know how to retain Jesus. Be lowly and peace-making and Jesus will be with you. Be devout and quiet and Jesus will stay with you. You can soon drive Jesus away, and lose his influence, if you determine to turn towards external things. And if you drive him away and lose him, to whom will.you fly, and whom will you then seek as a friend? You cannot very well live without a friend, and if Jesus is not your friend beyond all, you will be exceedingly sad and lonely. So you act like a fool if you trust or delight in any other. It were a better choice to have the whole world against us than to have Jesus hurt. Therefore of all dear ones let Jesus alone be specially loved.

Love all because of Jesus, but Jesus for himself. Jesus Christ alone is to be loved uniquely, he who before all friends is alone found good and faithful. Through him and in him let friends as well as foes be dear to you: and for all these he is to be entreated that they may all know and love him. Never wish to be singularly praised, for that alone is God's, who has none like himself. Nor wish that anyone should set his heart on you, nor that you should be possessed by a love for any other, but let it be Jesus in you, and in every good man.

Be pure and free throughout, not bound up with any other creature. You must be stripped of all, and bring a clean heart to God, if you would be at leisure to see how sweet the Lord is. And truly you will not attain to this unless you are led and drawn by his grace, so that emptied and set free in all things you become at one with him, alone with the alone. For when God's grace comes to a man, then is he strong in every way: and when it withdraws then will he be poor and weak, and as one left only for the scourge. He should not be cast down at this, nor despair, but stand with a steady mind towards the will of God, and endure whatever comes to him for the glory of Jesus Christ: for after winter follows summer, after night the day returns, and after storm great calm.

9. Of the lack of all comfort

IT IS not difficult to ignore human help when there is divine. It is a great thing, yes, very great, to be able to lack both human and divine help: and to be able to bear the heart's exile cheerfully for the honour of God, and in no way to seek oneself, nor think of one's own deserts. What a great thing it is if when the gift comes you are blithe and devout. Longed for by all is that hour. He rides gently enough whom God's grace carries. And what wonder if he feels no burden who is supported by the all-powerful and led by the supreme guide?

We gladly keep something to comfort us, and a man is with difficulty stripped of self. The holy martyr Lawrence, with his priesthood, mastered the worldly because he looked down on all that seemed attractive in the world: and, through love of Christ, even bore patiently the taking from him of God's high priest Sixtus whom he loved so much. He rose in that above the love of a man to the love of the Creator, and chose the divine pleasure instead of human solace. So should you too learn to give up any close and dear friend for love of God, nor feel it deeply when a friend leaves you, knowing that we must all sometime be parted from each other.

A man must struggle much and long within himself before he fully learns to master self and turn his entire affection towards God. When a man relies on himself he soon slips into human comforts. But the true lover of Christ and eager follower of the virtues does not fall back on comforts, nor seek such sensuous delights, but manly exercises rather, and the undertaking of hard work for Christ.

When therefore spiritual comfort is given by God, receive it with gratitude, but know it to be God's gift, not your desert. Be not exalted, nor over glad, nor foolishly presume: but be the more humble because of the gift, more wary and more tentative in all your actions, since that hour will pass and the testing follow. When comfort is withdrawn do not immediately despair, but with humility and patience await the heavenly visitation: for God can give you again a yet fuller encouragement.

This is nothing new or strange to those who know God's way, for there was often the same kind of alternation in the great saints and ancient prophets. Whence one, feeling divine influence present, said, "In my abundance I said I shall never be moved." But with the influence gone he goes on to say, "Thou didst avert thy face from me, and I became disquieted." Yet in the midst of this he in no way despaired, but the more earnestly begs of the Lord, and says: "To thee O Lord will I cry and will entreat my God." In time he gains the fruit of his prayer and testifies that he was heard, saying, "The Lord heard and took pity on me: the Lord became my helper." But in what way? "Thou hast changed," he says, "my bewailing into joy, and enfolded me with gladness."

If thus it happened with great saints, we who are weak and poor must not despair if we are sometimes fervent and then again cold: for the spirit comes and goes at the good pleasure of his will. Whence blessed Job says, "Thou visitest him at daybreak, and suddenly provest him."

On what then can I rely, or in whom should I trust, except in the great mercy of God alone, and in the sole hope of heavenly grace? For whether good men are about me, whether devout brothers or faithful friends, whether holy books or beautiful treatises, or sweet chants or hymns, all these help little, have small relish, when I am deserted by grace and left to my own poverty. Then indeed there is no better remedy than patience and self-submission to God's will.

I never found any, however religious and devout, who had not sometimes a withdrawal of grace, or who had not felt a lessening of fervour. Never was saint so highly rapt and illumined who first or last was not put to the test. For he is unworthy of the lofty contemplation of God who is not trained for God by some tribulation. For trial coming first is usually a sign of the consolation that follows. For to those tried by temptations celestial solace is promised. "He who overcomes," he says, "to him will I give to eat of the tree of life."

But divine comfort is given that a man may be stronger to hold up under adversities. And temptation follows lest he become conceited about his goodness. The devil sleeps not, nor is the flesh dead as yet: therefore cease not to prepare yourself for the fight, for to right and left are foes who never rest.

10. Of thankfulness for God's grace

WHY LOOK for rest when you were born to work? Adjust yourself to endurance rather than to comforts, and to the bearing of a cross rather than to pleasure. For who in the world would not willingly receive spiritual comfort and happiness if he could always get it? Because spiritual comforts exceed all the delights of the world and sensual pleasures. For all worldly delights are either hollow or base. Spiritual delights alone are really pleasing and honest, born of virtues, and infused by God into clean minds. But no one can enjoy these divine aids as he would like, for the testing time is never far away.

Now, apparent mental liberty and great self-assurance are largely against celestial visitation. God means well in giving the grace of consolation, but man does badly in not repaying all to God with an act of thankfulness. And so the gifts of divine influence cannot spring up in us because we are ungrateful to the giver, and do not pour all back again to the original source. For grace will always be added to the truly grateful, and what is usually given to the humble will be taken away from the proud.

I want no comfort that takes the sting of penitence from me. Nor do I aim at thought which leads to pride. For not everything high is holy, nor all the sweet good, nor every desire pure, nor every affection pleasing to God. Willingly do I accept the grace by which I may always be found lowlier and more reverent, and be made readier to give up myself.

One learned in the gift of grace, and schooled by the chastening of its withdrawal will not dare to attribute any good to himself, but rather confesses himself poor and bare. Give to God what is God's, and ascribe to yourself what is yours: that is, give to God the gratitude for grace, but to yourself the blame alone, and feel yourself punished rightly for the fault. Set yourself always in the lowest place, and you may be given the highest, for the highest does not exist without the lowest.

The saints highest before God are lowest in their own sight. And the more their glory, the deeper their humility. Full of heaven's truth and glory, they are not eager for empty praise. Rooted and strengthened in God, they cannot in any way be elated. And they who ascribe to God whatever good they have received will not look for another's praise, but long for the glory that is God's alone, and desire that God may be praised beyond everything in themselves and in all the saints; they tend ever to the Self-same.

Therefore be grateful for the least thing, and you will be fit to receive the greater. Let the least be to you just as the greatest, and the more contemptible be as of peculiar worth. If you peer into the excellence of the giver, no gift will seem small or worthless. For that is no slight thing which is given by the most high God. Even if he should give pains and chastenings there must be thanks, for whatever he allows to come upon us always makes for our welfare. He who wishes to keep God's favour, should be grateful for grace given, patient at its withdrawal. Let him pray that it may return: let him be careful and submissive lest it be lost.

11. Of the fewness of the lovers of the cross of Jesus

JESUS HAS many lovers of his heavenly kingdom now, but few bearers of his cross. He has many seekers of comfort, but few of tribulation. He finds many companions of the table, but few of abstinence. All are anxious to rejoice with him; few wish to endure anything for him.

Many follow Jesus as far as the breaking of bread, but few so far as to drink the chalice of suffering. Many revere his miracles, few pursue the ignominy of a cross. Many love Jesus so long as no adversities touch them. Many praise and bless him so long as they receive some comforts from him. But if Jesus hides himself and leaves them awhile, they fall into complaining or into extreme dejection. But those who love Jesus for Jesus himself, and not for some personal comfort of their own, speak well of him through every trial and heart-felt stress just as in the highest consolation. Even if he were never to give them comfort, they would still always praise him, and at all times would give thanks.

O how powerful is a pure love of Jesus, never confused with one's own gain or desire. Are they not all to be called hirelings who are always looking for comforts? Are they not proved lovers of self more than of Christ who are always studying their own convenience and gain?

Where will such a one be found who is ready to serve God for nothing? Rarely is any found so spiritual that he lives stripped of all. For who can find one truly poor in spirit and deprived of every created thing? Far and beyond the utmost limit is his worth. If a man would give all his substance, yet that is nothing: and if he should do a grievous penance, yet it is little: and if he should apprehend all knowledge, still he is far away: and if he should have a high character, and a very ardent devoutness, yet much is lacking in him, especially one thing most necessary for him.

What is this? That by letting everything go he should surrender himself and pass utterly out of self, and retain nothing of personal desire. And when he has done all that he knows should be done, let him feel he has done nothing, not thinking much of what might be considered great, but calling himself with truth an unprofitable servant: as the Truth says, "When you have done all that you are commanded, say, we are unprofitable servants.'' Then he may be truly poor and needy in spirit: and say with the prophet ''because I am solitary and poor''. Yet none is richer, none stronger, none freer than he who knows how to give up self and everything, and to put himself in the lowest place.

12. Of the royal road of the holy cross

HARD TO many seems this word, deny thyself, take up thy cross, and follow Jesus. But far harder will it be to hear that final word, depart from me ye cursed into everlasting fire. For those who readily hear and follow out the word of the cross now, will not then be afraid of hearing about the never-ending condemnation. This sign of the cross will be in the heavens, when the Lord comes to judge. Then all the servants of the cross who conformed themselves in life to the crucified will approach Christ the judge with great confidence.

Why therefore fear to bear a cross by which you come into a kingdom? In a cross is safety, in a cross is life, in a cross protection from foes, in a cross a flood of supernal sweetness, in a cross is mental strength, in a cross is spiritual joy, in a cross the height of courage, in a cross perfection of holiness. There is no safety of soul nor hope of eternal life but in the cross.

Therefore take up your cross and follow Jesus, and you will go on to life eternal. He went on before bearing his cross, and on the cross he died for you, that you too should carry your cross, and be ready to die on the cross. For if you should die with him, you will also in the same way live with him. And if you should be a sharer of the pain, you will also be of the glory too.

Lo, all stands on a cross, and all lies in the dying, and there is no other road to life and to true inward peace but the way of the holy cross and of daily dying to self. Walk where you will, seek whatever you will, and you will find no higher way above, nor safer way below than the way of the holy cross. Settle and order everything by your wish and outlook, yet you will always come upon something to be endured, either willingly or unwillingly, and so find ever a cross.

For either you will feel pain in the body, or sustain a troubled spirit in the soul. Sometimes you will be left as without God, sometimes upset by a neighbour: and, what is more, you will often be a burden to your very self; and you cannot be set free or eased by any cure or comfort, for while God wills it you must bear it. For God wishes you to learn to suffer trial uncomforted, and to cast yourself entirely upon him, and become the lowlier through the test. No one so heartily feels the suffering of Christ as he to whom it falls to suffer the like. Therefore a cross is always ready, and awaits you everywhere. You cannot escape it wherever you run, for wherever you go you carry self with you, and will always find it is your self. Look above, look below, look without, look within, and every way you will find a cross, and must keep yourself patient in every circumstance, if you would have inward peace, and win an everlasting crown.

If you carry a cross willingly it will carry you, and lead you to the wished-for end where there will surely be an end to suffering, though that will not be here. If you carry it unwillingly you make a burden for yourself, and load yourself the more, and still have to bear it. If you throw aside one cross you will certainly find another, and perhaps a heavier. Do you expect to evade what no mortal could escape? Which of the saints lived on earth without cross or trouble? For not even our Lord Jesus Christ was a single hour without the pain of suffering as long as he lived. Christ had to suffer, it says, and rise again from the dead, and so to enter into his glory. And how would you seek any other way than this royal road which is the way of the holy cross. Christ's entire life was a cross and a witnessing: and do you ask for rest and joy for yourself?

You are wandering, straying, if you look for aught else than to bear troubles, for all this mortal life is full of sorrows and marked round with crosses. And the higher one has advanced spiritually, the heavier far are the crosses he frequently finds, because the pain of his exile grows keener with love.

Yet such a man, dispirited in so many ways, is not without uplifting consolation, for he beholds the richest fruit grow for him out of the bearing of his cross. For while he willingly submits himself to it every troublous burden is changed into an assurance of divine comfort. And the more his body is worn with affliction, the more fully his spirit is strengthened by grace within. And sometimes he is so much stronger through enduring trouble and adversity for love of its resemblance to Christ's cross that he would not be without sorrow and trial, because he believes himself so much more precious to God, the more and heavier burdens he can bear for him.

It is not the strength of a man, but the influence of Christ, this which can and does so much in a frail body: so that what it natively hates and flies from, this it runs to, and loves with the soul's ardour. It is not man's nature to carry a cross, to love a cross: to chasten the body and subject it to servitude: to avoid honours, to bear insults steadily, to look down on self, and to prefer to be looked down upon: to face adversities and losses, and to desire no good fortune in this world. If you are centred on self you cannot of yourself be like this. But if you trust in the Lord, heavenly fortitude will be given you, and world and flesh be subject to your control. Nor will you fear a hostile devil if you are armed with faith and sealed with the cross of Christ.

Determine therefore as a good and faithful servant of Christ to carry manfully your Master's cross, crucified for you out of love. Prepare yourself to bear many misfortunes and varied discomforts in this unhappy life, for so it will be with you wherever you are, and so in fact you would find wherever you hid. It must be so: and there is no means of escape from the trouble of evils and sorrow than that you should endure through. Drink the Master's cup with a will, if you wish to be his friend and to share with him. Leave comforts to God: let him deal with such things as best pleases him. Set yourself indeed to bear trials and count them greatest comforts: for the sufferings of this present hour, even if alone you could sustain them all, are not worth comparing with future glory.

When you reach this point, that trial is a delight, and relished on Christ's account, then reckon it to be well with you, because you have found a paradise on earth. So long as it is hard for you to suffer and you try to escape, so long will you have no ease, and flight from trouble will follow you everywhere. If you fix your mind on what you ought, namely, on suffering and dying, it will soon be better with you, and you will find peace. Even if you were carried away into the third heaven with Paul, you are not certain, because of that, of suffering no adversity. "I," said Jesus, "will show him how much he must suffer for my name."

It remains therefore for you to suffer, if it is your delight to love Jesus and serve him perpetually. If only you were worthy of enduring something for the name of Jesus, what great glory would await you, what rejoicing among all God's holy ones, and what a help too it would be for anyone near you. For all praise endurance, but very few are willing to endure. You ought justly to suffer cheerfully a little for Christ when many suffer heavier things for the world.

Realise for a certainty that you ought to lead a dying life. And the more anyone dies to self so much the more he begins to live for God. No one is fit to lay hold of the heavenly unless he yields himself up to bear adversities for Christ. Nothing is more welcome to God, nothing more invigorating for you in this world, than to suffer willingly for Christ. And if choice were yours, you should rather choose to endure adverse things for Christ than to be refreshed with many comforts, because you would more resemble Christ, and be more like all the saints. For our worth, and the condition of our progress, does not rest on the many pleasant and consoling things, but rather on our pressing forward with great burdens and troubles.

If indeed there could be anything better and more helpful to men's well-being than to suffer, surely Christ would have shown it by word and example. For both to the disciples who followed him and to all who desire to follow him, he clearly urges the carrying of a cross, and says, "If anyone would come after me, let him deny himself and take up his cross and follow me." Therefore when all has been read through and searched into, let this be the ultimate conclusion: that through many tribulations we must enter into the kingdom of God.

BOOK III

OF INWARD CONSOLATION

BOOK III

OF INWARD CONSOLATION

1. Of Christ speaking inwardly to the faithful soul

I WILL listen to what the Lord God will say within me. Blessed is the soul that hears the Lord speaking within her, and receives a word of comfort from his mouth. Blessed are the ears which catch the pulsings of the divine whisper, and pay no heed to the murmurings of this world. Blessed indeed are the ears which heed no sound of voice outside, but truth teaching within. Blessed are the eyes which are closed to the outward, but are intent on the inward. Blessed are they who pass through to internal things, and by daily exercises strain to prepare themselves more and more to master heavenly secrets. Blessed are they who find time for God, and shake off every earthly impediment.

Mark these my soul, and shut the door of the senses so that you will hear what the Lord your God will speak within you. This thy beloved says: "I am thy safety, thy peace and thy life. Dwell with me and you will find peace." Put away all transitory things: seek those eternal. What are all temporal things, but deceitful? And what can all created things avail if you are left alone by the creator? Renounce all then, and make yourself pleasing and faithful to your creator so that you may be able to lay hold of true bliss.

2. *That truth speaks inwardly without the din of words*

SPEAK, LORD for thy servant hears. I am thy servant: give me understanding that I may know thy verities. Incline my heart to the words of thy mouth, that thy speech may distil as dew. The sons of Israel said to Moses of old, "Speak to us and we will listen: let not the Lord speak to us, lest perchance we die." Not so Lord do I pray, but rather, with the prophet Samuel, I humbly and earnestly implore, "Speak Lord, for thy servant hears."

Let not Moses speak to me, or any of the prophets, but speak to me thou, Lord God, inspirer and enlightener of all prophets, for thou alone without them canst perfectly fill me, but they without thee can effect nothing. They indeed can sound out words, but the spirit they cannot give. Beautifully do they speak, but with thee silent they inflame not the heart. They bring forth the writings, but thou openest the meaning. They put forward mysteries, but thou bringest knowledge of the things sealed. They state commands, but thou helpest the fulfilment of them. They point the way, but thou givest strength to walk in it. They work only from the outside, but thou dost prepare and illumine the heart. They water the surface, but thou givest fertility. They proclaim the words, but thou givest understanding to the hearers.

Let then no Moses speak to me, but thou, O Lord God, truth everlasting, lest perchance I die and prove fruitless through being thus admonished from without and not kindled from within: lest my judgment be the word heard and not done, known and not loved, believed and not kept. Speak therefore Lord, for thy servant hears, for thou hast the words of eternal life. Speak to me for some comforting of my soul, and for the amending of my whole life, and for thy praise and glory and perpetual honour.

3. That the words of God should be heard with humility and that many do not weigh them

SON, HEAR my words, sweetest of words, going beyond the knowledge of all the philosophers and wise men of this world. My words are spirit and life: not to be weighed by human reason. They are not to be brought out for mere pleasure, but to be heard in silence, and to be taken up with utter humility and great affection.

And I said: Blessed is he whom thou trainest, O Lord, and teachest him about thy law, that thou mayst make it easier for him in evil times, and he not feel alone on earth.

The Lord said: I taught the prophets from the beginning, and until now I cease not to speak to all, though many are deaf and yield not to my voice. Many listen more readily to the world than to God: they follow their fleshly desires more easily than God's good pleasure. The world offers petty and temporal things, and is served with great eagerness: I offer things high and eternal, and the hearts of mortals grow numb.

Who serves and obeys me with such care in everything as the world and its masters are served? "Blush, Sidon: says the sea." And if you ask the cause: hear why. For a modest living a long road is run: for living eternally scarce once will a foot be lifted from the ground by many. The paltriest wage is striven for, there is disgraceful quarrelling sometimes over a single coin: for a frivolous thing and a petty expectation they are not afraid to wear themselves out day and night: yet, Oh the shame of grudging the least fatigue for a changeless good, for a priceless gain, for highest honour, for endless glory.

Be heartily ashamed, you lazy and grumbling servant, that these are found readier for what must be lost than you for life. They are more joyful over an empty show, than you over reality. They indeed are sometimes disappointed in their hope, but my promise misleads no one, nor sends away empty him who trusts in me. What I have promised, I will give: what I have said, I will fulfil, if only anyone remains faithful in love of me right to the end. I am the rewarder of all the good, and the firm approver of all the devout.

Write my words on your heart, and earnestly dwell on them, for they will be very necessary in the hour of temptation. What you do not understand when you read, you will know at the time of my coming. I am wont to visit my chosen ones in two ways, namely by testing and by comforting. And I read two lessons to them daily: one, rebuking their faults, the other urging to growth in virtues. He who has heard my words, and despises them, has one who will judge him at the last day.

A prayer begging for the grace of devotion

O Lord my God, to me thou art all that is good. But who am I that I should dare to speak to thee? I am thy poorest little servant and a despicable little worm: far more poor and contemptible than I know and dare to say. Yet remember me O Lord, for I am nothing, have nothing, and can avail nothing. Thou alone art good, just and holy: thou canst do all, thou givest all, thou fillest all, leaving only the sinner empty.

Be mindful of thy mercies, and fill my heart with thy grace, thou who wouldst not have thy work be void. How can I sustain myself through this sad life unless thou fortify me with thy mercy and grace? Turn not thy face from me: delay not thy coming: withdraw not thy comfort: lest my soul become as unwatered land before thee.

O Lord teach me to do thy will: teach me to walk worthily and humbly before thee: for thou art my wisdom who truly knowest me, and knew me before the world was made, and before I was born into the world.

4. *That one should live with truth and humility in God's sight*

Son, walk before me in truth, and seek me always with the sincerity of your heart. He who walks with truth in my presence will be secure against invading evils, and truth will keep him free from false leaders and from the slanders of the unjust. If truth shall have set you free you will be free indeed, and you will not trouble about the hollow words of men.

Lord, it is true. As thou sayest, so I pray it may be with me. May thy truth teach me, itself guard me, and keep me safe right to the end. May it liberate me from every wrong feeling and disordered love, and I shall walk with thee in large freedom of heart.

I will teach you, Truth says, the things that are right and pleasing in my sight. Look on your sins with intense displeasure and sorrow, and never think anything of yourself for good works done. Most truly you are a sinner, both liable to and entangled with many passions. Of yourself you are always moving towards nothingness, easily wavering, easily overcome, easily bewildered, easily dissolved. You have nothing to boast of, but many things for which to count yourself worthless since you are far weaker than you can realise. So of all you do nothing should seem great to you.

Let nothing seem grand, nothing priceless and marvellous, nothing deserving fame, nothing lofty, nothing truly praiseworthy and desirable, except what is eternal. Let eternal Truth please you beyond all: your utter worthlessness be always displeasing to you. Nothing so fear, so blame and avoid, as your vices and sins which should displease you more than any losses of material things.

Some do not walk frankly with me, but, led by certain curiosity and conceit, wish to know my secrets and to grasp the far-off things of God, heedless of themselves and their well-being. These, with me against them, often fall into great temptations and sins through their pride and inquisitiveness.

Fear God's judgments: dread the anger of omnipotence. Yet do not question the doings of the Most High, but examine well your own shortcomings, in how many ways you have failed, and what many good opportunities you have ignored.

Some carry their devoutness only in books, some in images, and some in outward marks and forms. Some have me on their lips but little in their heart. Others there are who with enlightened mind and purified affection strain ever towards the eternal, listen wearily to talk about earthly concerns, and regretfully submit to nature's necessities: these feel what the spirit of truth utters within them, for it teaches them to look down on the earthly, and to love the heavenly: to disregard the world, and long for heaven the whole day and night.

5. Of the wonderful effect of divine love

I BLESS thee, heavenly Father, Father of my Lord Jesus Christ, because thou hast deigned to remember poor me. Thanks be thine, O Father of mercies, and God of all consolation, who hast at times given new life by thy comfort to me, one unworthy of any ease. I ever bless and glorify thee, with thine only-begotten Son and the Holy Spirit the comforter, for ever and ever.

Ah Lord God, my holy lover, when thou comest into my heart all my inward powers rejoice. Thou art my glory and the exultation of my heart. Thou my hope and my refuge in the day of my trouble. But because I am still feeble in love and imperfect in virtue I need to be strengthened and comforted by thee. Therefore come to me often and prepare me by holy disciplines: free me from evil passions: and heal my heart of all disordered feelings, so that, thoroughly cured and cleansed within, I may be made quick in love, strong in suffering, steady in perseverance.

Love is a great thing, a great good in every way: that alone makes every burden light, and leads smoothly over all unevenness. For it carries a load without being burdened, and makes every bitter thing sweet and savoury. The excelling love of Jesus impels to great deeds, and even excites to more perfect longings. Love would be on high, not held back by anything low. Love would be free, and estranged from every earthly feeling, lest its inner vision should be clouded, and itself be held in bonds by any temporal gains, or overcome by want. Nothing is sweeter than love, nothing stronger, nothing higher, nothing wider: nothing more delightful, nothing fuller nor better in heaven and earth: for love is born of God and cannot rest but in God beyond all things made.

The lover flies, runs, and rejoices: he is free and not to be held. He gives all for all, and has all in all, because he rests in the one highest beyond all, from whom all good springs and flows. He does not look at gifts, but beyond every good thing turns himself to the giver.

Love often knows no limit, but burns beyond every bound. Love feels no burden, reckons no toil, aims beyond its strength, never speaks of impossibility because it holds that all things are possible and allowable to it. Therefore it is capable of everything, and completes many things, being confident of the result, where one without love loses courage and gives up.

Love keeps watch, and sleeping slumbers not, wearied is not worn out, pressed is not depressed, deterred is not confounded, but like a living flame and burning torch it breaks its way upward and passes safely through. If anyone loves, he knows what this voice cries. A mighty cry it is in the ears of God, that ardent feeling of the soul which says, My God, my love, thou art all mine and I all thine.

Enlarge me in love that I may learn to taste with the inward mouth of the heart how sweet it is to love, and to dissolve and bathe in love. Let me be upheld by love, passing beyond self in very fervour and surprise. May I sing love's song, may I follow thee my beloved to the height: may my soul exulting with love lose itself in thy praise. May I love thee more than myself, nor myself except for thee, and in thee all who truly love thee: as the law of love shining from thee commands.

Love is alert, frank, duteous, cheerful and pleasing: brave, patient, faithful, prudent, long-suffering, manly, and never seeking self. For wherever anyone seeks self, there he falls away from love. Love is watchful, lowly and upright: not soft, nor frivolous, nor set on empty things: sober, chaste, steady, quiet, and keeps guard over all the senses. Love is submissive and obedient to prelates, poor and despised to itself, devout and thankful to God: always trusting and hoping in him even when God is not felt within him, for there is no living in love without pain.

He who is not ready to suffer anything, and to stand to the will of the beloved, does not deserve to be called a lover. A lover must take willingly every hardship and bitterness for the sake of the beloved, and not turn away from him because of chance opposition.

6. Of the test of a true lover

SON, YOU are not yet a strong and purposeful lover.

Why, Lord?

Because before a little opposition you give up the attempt and too eagerly look round for a solace. The brave lover stands firm through trials, and consents to no cunning persuasions of an enemy. As I please him in prosperity so I do not displease him in adversity. The wise lover does not so much consider a gift from the beloved, as the love of the giver. He turns to the feeling rather than the value, and sets all gifts below the one loved. The noble-minded lover builds not on the gift, but on me above every gift. So that all is not lost if you sometimes feel less deeply towards me and my saints than you would. That full and sweet affection which you know at times is the result of a moment's grace, and something of a foretaste of the celestial country. Do not depend too much on it, for it goes and comes. But to fight against the attacks of evil impulses on the mind, and spurn them as suggestions of the devil, is a sign of power and of great merit.

Therefore let no outlandish phantoms trouble you in whatever shape they come. Hold your purpose firmly with a straight intent towards God. It is no illusion when you are at times suddenly borne to the height and as quickly brought back to the heart's usual follies. For these you bear with rather than set in action, and so long as they do not satisfy you, and you resist them, it becomes a gain and not a loss.

Recognise that the old foe tries in every way to hinder your longing for goodness, and to keep you from every devout exercise, from reverence for the saints, from the pious remembrance of my suffering particularly, from useful recollection of sins, from the care of one's own heart, and from any strong resolve to advance in virtue. He inserts many evil thoughts that he may cause you lassitude and fear, and draw you away from prayer and holy reading. Humble confession annoys him, and if he could he would make you cease communion.

Neither believe nor heed him, however often he may lay deceiving snares for you. Charge him when he produces evil and unclean thoughts. Say to him, Go unclean spirit, blush for shame you wretch: you are most impure to bring such thoughts to my ears. Depart from me, most wicked deceiver, you shall not have any place in me, but Jesus will stay with me as a strong warrior, and you shall stand confounded. I would rather choose death and the bearing of uttermost pain than agree with you. Be silent and dumb: I will listen no more to you, though you may cause me many anxieties. The Lord is my light and my safety: whom shall I fear. The Lord is my helper and my redeemer.

Fight as a good soldier, and if sometimes you fall through weakness, resume energy more strongly than before, sure of my ampler grace: also be more on guard against self-pleasing and over-confidence. By these many are led astray, and sometimes fall into an almost incurable blindness. Let the fall of those proud ones who foolishly rely on themselves be a warning to you and a continuous humility.

7. *Of hiding grace under the guard of humility*

Son, it is better and safer for you to hide the grace of devotion, not to be too uplifted, nor speak much of it, nor to think too much about it, but rather to think little of yourself, and to be timid about the gift as coming to one undeserving. There is no inherent hold on this devout emotion, for it can quickly change to the opposite. When in grace remember how unhappy and helpless you usually are when without grace.

Progress in spiritual life is not so much at the time when you have its comforting grace, as when humbly, and self-lessly, and patiently you endure its withdrawal: so long as you are not then listless in the practice of prayer, nor allow your other accustomed duties to slide in any way, but do cheerfully what is in you, as you best can and know, and do not neglect yourself entirely because of any dryness or mental hesitation you feel. For there are many who become at once impatient or idle when things do not go well with them. A man's path is not always in his own power, and it is for God to give and to comfort whenever he will, and as much as he will, and to whom he will, as it pleases him and no more.

Some unwise ones have brought themselves down through

the grace of devotion because they wished to do more than they were equal to, not weighing the sum of their own littleness, but following the heart's prompting more than the judgment of reason. And because they assumed more largely than was pleasing to God they quickly lost his aid. They who placed a nest for themselves in heaven were made helpless and left low in order that humiliated and impoverished they might learn to fly not with their own wings but trusting in my feathers.

Those who are as yet new and inexperienced in the Lord's way can easily be misled and broken down, unless they rule themselves by the advice of the prudent. For if they choose to follow their own judgment rather than trust in the experience of others, the issue will be dangerous for them if they still refuse to be drawn back from their own conceit. Rarely will those who are a wisdom to themselves humbly allow others to rule them.

It is better to know a little with humility and with limited understanding, than to have great stores of knowledge with vain conceit. It is better for you to have a little, than a great deal which only makes you proud. He does not act with sufficient discretion who gives himself wholly to enjoyment, oblivious of his original helplessness, and the pure fear of the Lord which dreads losing a proffered grace.

Nor is he manly enough in mind who in the hour of adversity or of some depression surrenders utterly to despair, thinking over and feeling less trustfully of me than he should. He who in time of peace fixes his mind on being most secure, will often be found in time of war most dejected and full of fear. If you knew how to be always lowly and self-controlled, and also how to tame and rule your soul thoroughly, you would not fall so quickly into danger and stumbling.

Good advice it is, that in the birth of the soul's fervour you should keep in mind what the future may be with that light gone. And when that happens, remember that the light which I withdrew for a time as a warning to you and for my glory, can return anew. Such a testing is often more helpful than if you always had things prosper as you wish. For deserts are not reckoned by whether one has many visions or comforts, or is expert in scriptures, or is placed on a higher stage; but if he is grounded in true humility and filled with divine love, if he always seeks God's honour, purely and entirely, if he accounts himself nothing and actually despises self, and even rejoices at being looked down upon and humiliated by others more than at being honoured.

8. *Of low esteem of oneself before the eyes of God*

I WILL speak to my Lord, though I may be dust and ashes. If I consider myself more, lo, thou standest over against me, and my wrong-doings pronounce true evidence, nor can I contradict. But if I abase myself, and bring myself to nothing, and clear away all self-esteem, and grind myself to the dust I am, thy favouring grace will be mine, and thy light close to my heart, and all my self-esteem, even the least, shall be drowned in the vale of my nothingness, and perish for ever. There thou showest me to myself, what I am, what I was, and what I have come to: for I am nought and knew it not.

If I am left to myself, behold the nothingness and utter weakness. But if suddenly thou lookest on me, I am once made strong, and filled with new gladness. And, most wonderful it is that I am so instantly lifted up, and so graciously enfolded by thee, I who of my own weight sink always to the depths.

Thy love does this, coming freely to me first, and coming with help in so many needs: guarding me too from serious perils, and snatching me, as I may truly say, from innumerable evils. For indeed in wrongly loving self I lost myself: and in searching for thee alone, and in loving purely, I found alike myself and thee, and through love brought myself again the more profoundly to nothing. Because thou, O sweetest, dealest with me beyond all deserving, and beyond that which I dare hope or beg.

Blessed be thou my God: for though I be unworthy of all the good things, yet thine excelling and measureless goodness never ceases to do good even to the graceless, and to those far averse from thee. Turn us back to thee, that we may be thankful, lowly, and devout, for thou art our safety, our fortitude and strength.

9. *That all things must be referred to God as to final purpose*

SON, I ought to be thy supreme and ultimate purpose if you truly long to be blessed. By this intent your love will be purified, that love so often wrongly turned in on self and created things. For if you seek your self in anything, you immediately weaken and dry up within. Therefore refer all things to me firstly, for I am he who gave all. So consider each thing as flowing down from the highest good, and therefore to me as to their source all things are to be traced.

From me the tiny and the great, the poor and rich, as from a living fountain draw living water: and they who instinctively and cheerfully serve me shall receive grace for grace. But he who would glory in aught but me, or find delight in any personal gain, will not be established in true joy, nor be enlarged in his heart, but be hindered and straitened in many ways. For you ought to ascribe no good to yourself, nor attribute goodness to any man, but give all to God without whom man has nothing. I gave all, I will have all again, and with great strictness I ask for acts of thanksgiving.

This is a truth from which empty pride flies. And if celestial grace enters and true charity, there will be neither envy, nor hardness of heart, nor can self-love take possession.

For divine love overcomes all, and widens all the powers of the soul. If you rightly understand, you will rejoice in me alone, you will hope in me alone, for none is good save God alone, who above all is to be praised, and in all to be blessed.

10. That withdrawn from the world it is sweet to serve God

Now AGAIN will I speak Lord and not be silent, I will tell into the ears of my God, my Lord and my King, who dwells on high: O how great is the abundance of thy sweetness O Lord, which thou hast stored away for those that fear thee. But what art thou to those who love, what to those who serve with the whole heart? Truly ineffable the sweetness of thy contemplation, which thou hast given to those who love thee. In this hast thou most shown me the sweetness of thy love, that when I was not thou madest me, and when I strayed far from thee thou didst bring me back again to serve thee, and taught me to love thee.

O fount of constant love: what may I say of thee? How can I forget thee who deignest to remember me even when I was waste and spent? Thou hadst pity upon thy servant beyond all expectation, and showed favour and loving-kindness beyond all deserving.

What return can I make thee for such grace? For it is not given to all to renounce all, to give up the world, and to take up the monastic life. Is it any great thing that I should serve thee whom all creation is bound to serve? It should not seem much to me to serve thee, but this rather should seem great and marvellous to me, that thou dost stoop to accept in service one so poor and worthless, and to make him one with thy chosen servants. Lo all I have and by which I serve are thine.

Yet on the other hand thou servest me more than I thee. Behold heaven and earth which thou didst create for the service of man stand before thee and daily perform what thou orderest. And this is little, since thou hast placed even angels at the service of man. But this transcends all: that thou thyself deignest to serve man, and hast promised to give him thy very self.

What shall I give thee for all these thousandfold blessings? Would that I could serve thee all the days of my life. If only I could for but a single day show thee a fitting service. Truly thou art worthy of every act of service, every honour and eternal praise. Truly thou art my Lord, and I thy poor servant, one bound to serve thee with all my powers, nor ought I ever to grow weary in thy praises. So will I, so do I desire, and whatever is lacking in me deign thou to add.

Great the honour, great the glory to serve thee, and to make light of all for thy sake. For much grace will they have who willingly place themselves under thy most holy service. They who, for thy love, put aside all bodily enjoyment, will find sweetest solace from the holy spirit. Great freedom of mind will they gain who enter on the strait way for thy name, and pay no heed to all worldly interest.

O pleasant and joyous service of God by which a man is made truly free and holy. O holy state of religious bondage which makes a man equal to angels, pleasing to God, terrible to demons, and commendable to all the faithful. O welcome and ever-desirable service, which awards the highest good, and attains a joy that endlessly remains.

11. *That passionate longings are to be examined and restrained*

SON, YOU must still learn in addition many things which you have not yet thoroughly grasped.

What are these, Lord?

That you mould your desires entirely by my pleasure, and be not a lover of self, but an eager imitator of my will.

Desires often inflame and fiercely drive you, but note whether you are more moved for my honour or for your own gain. If I am the reason, you will be quite content with whatever I shall appoint. But if any self-seeking lurks there, lo, this it is that impedes and burdens you.

So beware lest you cling too closely to a pre-conceived wish without consulting me, in case that which at first pleased, and was keenly sought as being best, afterwards perhaps hurts or displeases. For every impulse which seems good is not to be obeyed at once: nor again is every opposite impulse to be shunned at the start.

It is sometimes wise to use the curb even over good endeavours and desires, lest through the mind's insistence you rush into perplexity, lest by lack of control you give rise to scandal among others, or else through their opposition you suddenly hesitate and fall back. Sometimes you must really use violence and manfully resist sensual appetite, not caring what the body wants or does not want, but aiming mainly at this, that, even against its will, it shall be subject to the spirit. And it should continue to be chastened and forced to submit to obedience until it is ready for anything, and learns to be content with little, and to love simple things, without murmuring against any discomfort.

12. *Of the growth of patience and the struggle against concupiscence*

LORD GOD, patience, as I see, is very necessary for me, because many things happen contrary in this life. For whatever I settle on for my own peace, my life cannot exist without warfare and sorrow.

Son, so it is. But I would have you seek no such peace as is void of trials or feels no opposition, but conclude rather that you have then found peace when you have been drilled by various troubles, and tested by many adversities. If you say you cannot stand much, how then will you endure the purging fire? Of two evils always choose the less. Struggle to bear present evils with a mind steadily set towards God, so that you may escape lasting future sufferings.

Do you think men of the world suffer nothing or little? You will not find it so, even if you question the most luxurious. But, you will say, they have many pleasures and follow their own wishes, and so their troubles lie light. Be it so, that they have whatever they want. But how long do you think it will last?

See, like smoke the world's rich men shall vanish, and there will remain no record of joys passed. Yes, even when they were still living, they had no peace in them without bitterness, weariness and fear. For they often drew the sting of pain from the very thing in which they conceived delight. It was right that because they sought and followed disordered pleasures they should not have their fill without disquiet and bitterness. Oh how short, how deceitful, how disorderly and base are all such pleasures. Yet they know not how drunk and blind they are, but like dumb beasts incur spiritual death for the sake of a little enjoyment in a fading life.

Therefore, son, go not after your lustful longings, but turn away from your wilfulness. Delight in the Lord and he will give you the prayers of your heart. For if you would really find enjoyment, and be abundantly consoled by me, see what your blessing will be in the disdain of all worldliness, and the cutting away of all base pleasures, and plenteous comfort will be given you. And the more you withdraw from the solace of every created thing, so you will find far more tender and powerful comforts in me.

But at first you will not reach these without a certain sadness and laborious fight. A rooted habit resists, but will be overcome by a better habit. Flesh will murmur, but be curbed by fervour of spirit. The old serpent will goad and incite you, but be driven off by prayer: and, best of all, his chief entry be closed by your doing some useful work.

13. Of lowly obedient submission after Jesus Christ's example

SON, HE who tries to escape from obedience withdraws himself from grace. And he who looks for private ends misses the common good. He who does not cheerfully and readily submit himself to his superior shows a sign that his flesh does not yet perfectly obey him, but often resists and complains. Therefore learn to submit yourself quickly to your superior if you would subjugate your bodily self. For the outer man is more swiftly beaten if the inner man is not laid waste.

There is no more troublesome and worse enemy of the soul than you yourself not thoroughly in accord with your spirit. You must in every way adopt a real contempt for self if you would hold out against flesh and blood. It is because you still love self too intensely that you hesitate to yield to the will of others.

Yet what great matter if you who are dust and nothingness submit yourself to a man for God's sake, when I, almighty and most high, subjected myself most humbly to man for you? I became humblest and lowest of all that you might conquer your pride by my humility.

Learn to obey, you dust: learn to humble yourself, you earth and clay, and to give way under all feet. Learn to break up your own desires and to yield yourself to every act of subjection. Be afire against self, allowing no pride to live in you, but show yourself as submissive and insignificant, that everyone can walk over you and tread you down like mud of the streets.

Trivial man, what have you to complain of: stained sinner, what can you reply to your accusers, you who have offended God so often, and deserved the lowest depths so many times? But because your soul was precious to my sight my eye was merciful to you, that you might understand my love,

and be always grateful for my good gifts: and that you might
give yourself up continually to true submission and humility,
and patiently acquire contempt of self.

14. Of keeping in mind God's hidden discernments lest we boast of our own goodness

THOU THUNDEREST thy decisions over me O Lord, and
shakest all my bones with fear and trembling, and makest my
soul deeply afraid. I stand astounded, turning the thought
over that the very heavens are not pure in thy sight. If thou
hast found perversity in angels yet did not spare them, what
will happen to me? Stars fell from heaven: what can I that
am dust expect? They whose works seemed laudable have
fallen to the depths, and I see those who ate the bread of
angels revelling in husks of swine.

Thus there is no sanctity if thou O Lord withhold thine
hand, no wisdom avails if thou cease to guide, no courage
helps if thou dost not defend, no chastity is safe if thou
protect it not, no guard of ours will serve if thy holy
vigilance be not there. For being left we sink and perish,
but being visited we are borne up and alive. We are
wavering indeed if not strengthened by thee, and lukewarm
when not inflamed by thee.

O how lowly and abjectly ought I to feel about myself,
and even if I seem to possess a goodness, to account it
nothing. O how deeply should I bow beneath thine unfathomable judgments O Lord when I find myself to be
naught else but nothing and a nobody. O measureless
thought, O impassable sea, where I find nought about myself but absolute nothingness.

Where then is pride's retreat: where the assurance born
of virtue? All empty boasting is absorbed in the depth of
thy judgments on me. What is all flesh in thy sight? Shall
the clay pride itself against him who shapes it? How can he
be uplifted with boastful talk whose heart is truly submissive

to God? The whole world could not bolster up one whom truth brings down under itself, nor will he whose whole hope is fixed on God be affected by a mouth full of flatteries. For even of those who speak, see how naught they all are, for they cease with the sound of the spoken words: but the truth of the Lord lasts for ever.

15. What to do and say about everything we wish for

SON, SPEAK in this way on every matter: Lord, if it please thee, so let this be done. Lord, if it be for thine honour, let this come about in thy name. Lord, if thou see it to be helpful to me, and know it to be for my good, then give me this to use for thy praise. But if thou knowest it to be bad for me, and no gain to the health of my soul, take such a desire from me. For every wish is not out of a holy spirit even though it may seem right and good to a man.

It is difficult to decide truly whether a good or a hostile influence impels you to this or that longing, or whether you are prompted by the spirit of self. Many have been deceived in the end, who, at the beginning seemed led by a good inspiration. Therefore whatever presents itself to the mind as desirable is always to be wished and prayed for with fear of God and lowliness of heart, and above all to be entirely left to me with self-resignation, saying: Lord thou knowest which is better: let this or that be done as thou wilt. Give what thou wilt, and as much as thou wilt, and when thou wilt. Use me as thou knowest best and as best pleases thee, and the greater will be thy praise. Place me where thou wilt, and deal freely with me everyway. I am in thy hand, turn and re-turn me on the winding way. See, I am thy servant, ready for anything because I do not wish to live for myself but for thee: would it might be worthily and perfectly.

Prayer for carrying out God's own pleasure

Give me thy grace, Jesu most kind, that it may live with me and work with me, and persist with me right to the end. Grant me this: always to wish and will what is most acceptable and dear to thee. Let thy will be mine, and my will always follow thine, and be in complete accord with it. May I be one with thee to will and not to will, unable to will or nill aught else, but as thou willest or willest not.

Grant me to die to all things that are in the world, and for thy sake to be put aside and unknown in this earthly time. Grant me beyond all things that can be desired to rest in thee, with my heart at peace in thee. Thou art the heart's true peace, thou the sole rest: apart from thee all things are hard and disquieting. In this peace, in the self-same, that is, in thee, the one supreme eternal good, will I lie down and rest. Amen.

16. That true solace is to be looked for in God alone

WHATEVER I can wish or imagine as my solace I do not expect here, but hereafter. For if I alone might have all earth's comforts, and could enjoy all its delights, I know they could not last long. Hence, soul of mine, you cannot be fully comforted nor perfectly refreshed except in God the consoler of the poor and sustainer of the lowly.

Wait a little, my soul: look towards the divine promise, and you will have abundance of all good things in heaven. If you make too eagerly for these present things you may lose the eternal and heavenly. Things of time are to be used, those of eternity to be desired. You cannot be satisfied with any temporal goods because you are not made simply to enjoy them.

Again, if you owned all good things created, you could not be happy and blessed: but only in God who created all does thy whole blessedness and happiness stand: not in what is seen and applauded by the foolish lovers of the world, but in what the good and faithful ones of Christ look for, and which the spiritual and pure in heart whose intercourse is in the heavenly, sometimes tasted beforehand. Vain and short-lived is all human solace. Blessed and true the solace which takes entire possession within by truth.

A devout man carries everywhere with him his comforter, Jesus, and says to him: Be present with me Lord Jesus in every place and time. May this be my consolation to be cheerfully willing to forego all human comfort. And if thy solace be withdrawn, let thy will and just probation of me be my chief comfort. For thou wilt not always chide, nor keep thine anger for ever.

17. *That every anxiety is to be referred to God*

SON, LET me do what I choose with you: I know what is best for you. You think as a man: you decide in many matters as human feeling prompts.

Lord, what thou sayest is true. Thine anxiety for me is greater than all the care I can take for myself. Most precariously he stands who does not throw all his disquietude upon thee. Lord if my will keeps upright and strong towards thee, do with me whatever pleases thee. For whatever thou doest with me cannot be other than good. If thou choose that I be in the shadows, blessed be thou: and if thou wilt that I be in the light, again be thou blessed. If thou deign to comfort me, blessed be thou: and if thou wilt that I be troubled, alike be thou ever blessed.

Son, thus must you bear yourself if you would walk with me. So should you be as ready to suffer as to rejoice. Thus should you as cheerfully be needy and poor as sated and rich.

Lord, readily will I endure for thee whatever thou willest to come upon me. Without distinction will I take from thy hand good and evil, sweet and bitter, joy and sadness, and give thanks for all that happens to me. Guard me from all sin and I will fear neither death nor hell. If only thou cast me not away for ever, nor efface me from the book of life, whatever trial sweeps over me shall not harm me.

18. *That temporal ills are to be calmly borne after Christ's example*

SON, I came down from heaven for your well-being: I took up your miseries not from necessity but drawn by love, so that you might learn patience, and, for the time, bear ills without rebelling. For from the hour of my birth even to the ending on the cross, I was never without the burden of sorrow. I had great lack of temporal things: I often heard many complaints about myself: I bore with good will troublous and abusive words: I received ingratitude for benefits, profanities for deeds of wonder, censures for teachings.

Lord, since thou wert patient throughout thy life, in this fulfilling perfectly the command of thy Father, it is right that I a poor little sinner should bear myself patiently in following thy will, and, so long as thou choosest for my welfare, endure the burden of a life that is spoiled. For though life now seems so heavy laden, yet it is already made deeply worthful by thy grace, and more bearable and intelligible by thine example, and the footsteps of thy saints: yes, and much more tranquil than once it was under the ancient law, when the gate of heaven was kept shut, and the very road to heaven seemed more hidden: when so few cared to seek the kingdom of heaven: and they too who at that time were upright and destined to be saved, could not enter the celestial realm before thy suffering and the obligation of holy death.

Oh what thanks am I bound to give thee because thou didst stoop to show me and all faithful ones the straight and good road into thine everlasting kingdom. For thy life is our road, and by holy patience we walk towards thee who art our crown. Unless thou hadst gone before and taught us, who would have troubled to follow? Ah, how many would have lingered far off and behind, unless they had seen thy splendid example. Lo, as it is, we remain unmoved, though hearing so much of thy wonders and teachings: what would happen if we had not such a light for following thee?

19. Of enduring things that hurt, and how true patience is tested

WHAT IS it you are talking of, son? Stop complaining, by thinking of my suffering and that of other saints. You have not yet withstood to the blood. It is little you suffer compared with those who bore so much, were so strongly tempted, so heavily afflicted, tried and harassed in so many ways. You should therefore bring to mind the heavier trials of others, that you may the easier bear your very trifling ones. And if they do not seem so small to you, look out, lest your impatience causes this. Yet whether they are small or great, strive to bear them all patiently. The better you yourself prepare for suffering, so much the wiser will you act, and the more amply gain: more easily too will you endure when you are actively prepared for this in mind and practice. Do not say, "I cannot put up with these things from such a man, and I ought not to stand things like this, for he did me great wrong, and charged me with what I never thought of, though I will cheerfully bear it from someone else as far as I think I ought to." Such a thought is childish, for it does not realise the strength of patience, nor by whom it will be crowned, but prefers to dwell on personalities, and on things set to its account that hurt.

He is not really patient who is only ready to suffer as much as he chooses for himself, and from whom he pleases.

But one who is truly patient does not mind by what man he is tried, whether by his prelate, or by someone equal or inferior, whether by a good and holy man, or by one bad and worthless: but from every creature alike, however much and often anything adverse happens to him, he takes it all from God's hand gratefully, and counts it great gain, for with God nothing, however small, if endured for him, can pass without reward.

So if you would gain victory be ready for the fight. You cannot attain the crown of patience without a struggle. If you will not bear the pain, you are refusing to be crowned. But if you long to be crowned, fight manfully, bear patiently. Without toil one does not reach rest, nor without fighting come to victory.

Lord may that be possible for me by grace which seems impossible to me by nature. Thou knowest how little I am able to suffer, and how quickly I am cast down at the rising of a slight adversity. Let each discipline of trouble be made lovely and desirable for thy name, since to bear pain and testing for thy sake is most salutary for my soul.

20. Of acknowledging one's own weakness and the ills of this life

AGAINST MYSELF I will declare my unrighteousness. I will confess my weakness to thee, O Lord. It is often a little thing that saddens and dejects me. I intend to act bravely, but when a small temptation appears, it becomes a great strain to me. Sometimes it is a mere trifle out of which a serious test arises. And when I reckon myself fairly safe, just when I am not thinking, I sometimes find myself almost overcome as by a light breath.

Therefore Lord, look on my lowliness and frailty, known in every way by thee; pity me and lift me out of the mire, that I sink not, nor remain for ever cast down. This it is that often repels and confounds me before thee, that I am so wavering and weak in resisting passions. And although I may not yield altogether, yet the taint of these things is trying and oppressive to me, and it is very wearing to live through daily conflict like this. By this my weakness is borne in upon me, that detested fancies always pour in more easily than they go out.

Most mighty God of Israel, inspirer of faithful souls, if thou wouldst but regard the toil and sorrow of thy servant, and aid him in all that he would carry through! Strengthen me with heavenly endurance, lest the primitive man, hapless flesh not yet subdued to the spirit, get the upper hand and domineer: against which I must struggle as long as I have breath in this troubled life.

Oh what sort of life is this, where troubles and ills are never absent, where everything is full of snares and foes? For when one trouble or temptation recedes, another enters: and even while one conflict goes on many others unexpectedly arrive. And how can life be loved that has so many bitternesses, and is exposed to so many adversities and distresses? How too can it be called life, giving birth to so many deadly and baneful things? Yet loved it is, and many seek after its allurement.

The world is often charged with being false and hollow, yet it is not easily given up, for fleshly desires dominate too much. But some things lead us to love it, some to despise it. Lust of the flesh, lust of the eyes, and the pride of life attract to a love of the world: but, as pains and ills justly follow these, they beget a hatred and disgust towards the world.

How sad it is that depraved pleasure overcomes a mind given to the world, so that it counts being among briars a delight, because it neither sees nor tastes the sweetness of God and the inner charm of virtue. But they who put the world completely aside, and under a holy discipline endeavour to live for God, these are not unaware of the divine delight promised to true renunciants, and they see how gravely and in what varied ways the world goes wrong and is deceived.

21. *That one should find rest in God beyond all good things and gifts*

BEYOND ALL things and in all things, my soul, rest in the Lord always, for he himself is the eternal rest of the holy.

Grant me most sweet and loving Jesus, to rest in thee beyond every creature: beyond all health and beauty, beyond all glory and honour, beyond all power and dignity, beyond all knowledge and subtlety, beyond all riches and arts, beyond all joy and exultation, beyond all fame and praise, beyond all pleasantness and comfort, beyond all hope and promise, beyond every merit and desire, beyond all gifts and rewards thou canst bestow and diffuse, beyond all gladness and rejoicing that mind can take and feel: yes, even beyond angels and archangels and all the heavenly host, beyond all things visible and invisible, and beyond all that thou my God art not.

For thou O Lord my God art supreme beyond all: thou alone most high, thou alone most mighty, thou alone all-sufficing and full, thou alone most sweet and consoling, thou alone most lovely and loving, thou alone most noble and glorious beyond all: in whom all good things at once and perfectly are, and always were, and will be, and therefore whatever thou givest me outside thyself, or revealest or promisest, while I see thee not nor fully understand, that same is little and unsatisfying. For indeed my heart cannot truly rest nor be entirely contented unless it rests in thee, and transcends all gifts and every creation.

O my most beloved spouse Jesus Christ, purest lover, ruler of all things made, who will give me the wings of true freedom to fly to thee and stay there? O when will it be granted me to be fully at leisure and see how sweet thou art, O Lord my God? When shall I find myself once more complete in thee, so that in love of thee I may not be conscious of myself, but of thee alone beyond all sense and bound, in a way not known to all. But now I often sigh, and bear my unhappiness with grief. For many evils meet me in this vale of troubles, and they often disturb, sadden, and overcloud me: often hinder and thwart, allure and entangle so that I cannot have free access to thee, nor enjoy the glad welcomes ever awaiting blessed spirits.

Let my sighs and great loneliness on earth move thee O Jesu, brightness of eternal glory, comfort of the pilgrim soul. My mouth is voiceless before thee: only my silence speaks to thee. How long will my Lord tarry in coming?

Let him come to me, his destitute one, and make me happy. Let him stretch out his hand and deliver a hapless one from every strait. Come, come: for without thee no day or hour will be happy, for thou art my joy, and without thee my table is bare. Poor am I, and as one imprisoned and loaded with fetters, till thou ｉrevive me with the light of thy presence and set me free, and show thy kindly face. Others may seek whatever else pleases instead of thee: naught else does or shall please me, but thou, my God, my hope, eternal welfare. I will not keep silence nor cease to pray till thy favour turn again and thou speak inwardly to me.

Behold, I am here: lo, I to you: because you called me. Your tears and your soul's yearning, your humiliation and contrition of heart have drawn me down and brought me to you.

And I said, Lord I called thee and longed to enjoy thee, ready to refuse everything for thee. For thou didst urge me first to seek thee. Blessed be thou for this O Lord, doing this good thing for thy servant, so like the multitude of they mercies.

What has thy servant more to say in thy presence but that he should deeply humble himself before thee, remembering always his own wrong-doing and worthlessness?

For there is none like thee in all the wonders of heaven and earth. Thy works are exceedingly good, thy decisions true, and thy forethought governs the universe.

Therefore praise and glory be thine, O Wisdom of the Father: let my mouth, my soul, and all things made, together praise and bless thee.

22. Of recounting God's manifold blessings

OPEN MY heart Lord to thy law, and teach me to walk in thy precepts. Help me to understand thy will, and with deep reverence and diligent thought to bear in mind thy kindnesses in general as well as in particular, so that for the future I may be able to return grateful thanks to thee worthily. I know well and acknowledge that I cannot even to the smallest point pay the praises that are due. Less am I than all the good Thou gavest me, and when I consider thine excellence my spirit fails before the magnitude.

All that we have in soul and body, and whatever we possess outwardly or inwardly, naturally or supernaturally, are thy blessings, and pronounce thee bounteous, just and good, from whom we receive all good things. Though one receives more, another less, yet all are thine, and one cannot have the least thing without thee. He who receives the greater cannot boast of his own deserving, nor lift himself above others, nor taunt the lesser: for greater and better is he who ascribes less to himself, and is more lowly and devout in returning thanks. And he who considers himself meaner than all and judges himself to be less worthy, is the more fit to receive greater things. Yet he who has received fewer should not be sad, nor take it complainingly, nor envy the better endowed, but should rather turn to thee and praise thy goodness the more for scattering thy gifts so richly, so freely and willingly, without taking note of individual desert. All comes from thee, and therefore thou art to be praised for everything.

Thou knowest what is best to give to each; and why this one should have less and that one more, is not ours to distinguish but thine who dost fix each one's merits. Whence, O Lord, I even count it a great blessing not to have much of what seems a worth and a glory outwardly and according to men, because anyone who reflects on his own poverty and paltriness should not feel a burden or sadness or dejection in it, but comfort and great blitheness instead, in that thou, God, hast chosen for thyself the poor and lowly and despised of this world as intimates and of thy household. Thine apostles themselves are witnesses, whom thou hast made princes over the whole earth: yet they lived in the world without complaining, so lowly and simple, utterly without an evil thought or pretence, and even rejoiced to suffer insults for thy name, and most passionately embraced what the world detests.

Truly nothing should so delight one who loves thee and knows thy kindnesses as thy will towards him, and the tenderness of thine eternal plan with which he ought to be so contented and satisfied that he would as willingly be least as another would wish to be greatest, and be as calm and contented in the last place as in the first, and as cheerfully be ignored and put aside as nameless and without repute, as be more honoured and greater in the world than others. For thy will, and the love of thy regard, should stand out beyond everything, and more comfort and better please him than all blessings bestowed or yet to be given.

23. Of four things that bring great peace

SON, NOW will I teach you the way of peace and true freedom.

Lord, do as thou sayest, for it gives me joy to hear this.

Try, son, to do the will of another rather than thine own. Always prefer to do with less than more. Always look for the lower place and be submissive to all. Always wish and pray that God's entire will may be brought to pass in you. For, see, such a man enters the confines of peace and rest.

Lord, this thy brief talk contains in itself many a perfection. Little is said, yet full of meaning and copious in fruit. For if it could be faithfully kept by me, unrest would not so easily arise in me. For as often as I feel myself disquieted and burdened, I find I have gone back from this teaching. But thou who canst do all, and carest always for my soul's good, add still the larger grace that I may be able to carry thy word through, and bring about my deliverance.

A prayer against evil thoughts

O Lord my God be not far from me: my God look down to help me: for strange thoughts and deep fears have risen up within me, afflicting my soul. How shall I get through unharmed? How shall I break them up? "I," he says, "will go before you, and will bring down the boasting sons of earth. I will open the prison doors, and will unveil the secret of mysteries to you."

Do as thou sayest Lord, and all wicked thoughts will fly at the sight of thee. This is my hope and only comfort: to fly to thee in every trouble, to rely on thee, to call to thee from the innermost, and patiently look for thy solace.

A prayer for enlightenment of mind

Good Jesus enlighten me with the clear shining of inward light, and take away every obscurity from my heart's dwelling. Restrain my many roaming thoughts, and crush the fierce assaults of temptations. Fight strongly for me and conquer the evil beasts, fleshly allurements, I mean, that there may be peace through thy power, and thine abounding praise resound through the holy temple, that is, in the clean conscience. Command the winds and storms: say to the sea, be still, and to the north wind, blow not, and there shall be great calm. Send out thy light and truth that they may shine over the earth, for worthless and useless clay am I unless thou illumine me. Pour thine influence from above, bathe my heart in heavenly dew, serve out to me streams of devotion to water the face of the earth, to bring forth the good and the finest fruit. Uplift a mind pressed down by a load of sins, and raise every desire of mine towards celestial ends, so that tasting the sweetness of supernal felicity I shall be ashamed to think much of the earthly. Haste and deliver me from all the fugitive comfort of creatures, for nothing made can fully console and quiet my longing. Unite me to thee with the inseparable bond of love, for thou alone satisfiest him that loves thee, and with thee away worlds are worthless.

24. *Of avoiding inquisitive curiosity about the life of others*

SON, BE not inquisitive, nor concerned with unreal troubles. What is this one or that to you: follow me. For what does it matter to you whether this one is such or such: or whether that one does or says so and so? You will not have to answer for others, but will render an account for your own self. Therefore why entangle yourself? Lo, I know all men, and see all that is done under the sun: and I know how it is with each one, what he thinks, what he wants, and towards what end his intent is set.

So, everything should be left to me, but do you keep yourself in goodly peace, and let the man easily moved busy himself as much as he chooses. Whatever he has done or said will fall upon him, for he cannot escape me.

Care not about the shadow of a great name, nor the close acquaintance of many, nor the personal affection of men. For these breed distractions and great misunderstandings in the heart. Freely would I utter my word to you and unveil hidden things, if you would carefully look out for my coming, and open the door of your heart to me. Use fore-sight, be alert in prayers, and humble yourself in every way.

25. *What settled peace of heart and true progress consist in*

SON, I have said, "peace I leave with you, my peace I give you, not as the world gives do I give you." All long for peace, but all do not care for what leads to true peace. My peace is with the humble and lowly of heart. Your peace will be through many forms of patience. If you hear me and follow my voice you will be able to enjoy much peace.

What then shall I do?

In everything look to yourself, what you do and what you say, and turn every intention of yours to this, that you may please me alone, desiring or seeking nothing outside me: but as to the sayings or actions of others, pass no flippant judgment, nor mix yourself up with matters not concerning you: thus doing you will be little or rarely perturbed. Yet never to feel any disquiet, nor suffer any trial of mind or body, is not a possibility of present time but of eternal rest.

Do not think then that you have found real peace when you feel no burden, nor that all is well with you when you suffer no opposition, nor assume that to be perfect when everything happens in accord with your liking; nor reckon yourself in any way great at such a time, nor consider yourself as specially beloved because you feel great devoutness and tenderness: for the true lover of virtue is not known by this, nor does the progress and perfection of a man rest on this. In what then, Lord?

In giving up yourself whole-heartedly to the divine will, in not seeking your own either in small or great, in time or eternity, so that with one steady outlook amid prosperity and adversity, weighing every event in an even balance, you continue to be grateful. If you can be so firm and enduring in hope that when the inward solace is withdrawn you can even then prepare your heart for further endurance, and not justify yourself as if you ought not to suffer these and suchlike things, but justify me in every circumstance, and praise the holiness of it: then will you walk in the true and straight path of peace, and know the undoubting hope of once again beholding my face with joy. For if you reach complete contempt of your very self, be sure that then you will enjoy as full a peace as any earthly pilgrim can.

26. Of the excellence of a free mind which is acquired by earnest prayer more than by study

LORD, THIS is the task of a perfect man, never to release the soul from straining after heavenly things, and, amidst many cares, to press on as if without a care, not in a listless way but with the certain assurance of a free mind, clinging to no created thing with unruly feeling.

My most gracious God, I beg thee lest I become too closely involved to keep me from the concerns of this life: from the body's many wants, lest I be caught by pleasure: from every obstacle of the soul, lest broken with anxieties I be overthrown. I do not speak of those things which earthly vanity feverishly courts, but of those ills which, as a curse of common mortality, a punishment, depress and hold back the soul of thy servant, lest he should be able to enter into spiritual freedom as often as he would.

O God, my ineffable sweetness, turn into bitterness for me every fleshly comfort that draws me from love of things eternal, and wickedly entices me by keeping in view some immediate fascinating interest. Do not let it conquer me, my God, nor overcome flesh and blood: let not earth and its brief glory cheat me, nor the devil and his cunning trip me up. Give me the fortitude to resist, the patience to endure, the constancy to persevere. Give the anointing of thy spirit rather than all the comforts of earth, and in place of carnal love pour in the love of thy name.

See how bread, drink, clothing, and other necessaries pertaining to the body's support, are burdensome to a fervent spirit. Make me use such supplies moderately, not caught by too much desire. One must not throw aside everything, for nature must be kept up. But the holy law forbids the asking for things superfluous and things that mainly give pleasure, for then the flesh rises insolently against the spirit. Amid these things I ask that thy hand may guide and show me, lest I assume too much.

27. That it is self-love chiefly that holds us back from the highest good

SON, YOU should give all for all, and be as nothing to yourself. Realise that your self-love hurts you more than anything in the world. In proportion to the love and feeling you have for anything so it clings to you more or less. If your love were pure, simple and well-controlled, you would not be enslaved by anything.

Do not covet what you ought not to have. Do not keep what may impede and rob you of freedom. It is strange that you do not commit yourself entirely to me from the depth of your heart, together with all you can wish for or possess.

Why use yourself up with vain regret? Why be worn out with superfluous cares? Stand firm for what pleases me and you will suffer no loss. If, in order to have more pleasure and gain of your own, you look for this or that, and want to be here or there, you will never be at rest or free from anxiety, because you will find some flaw in everything, and in every place someone who will be against you.

So that to obtain or multiply external things is no help: far better be indifferent and cut them radically out of the heart. This, you understand, not only means money-making and other wealth, but the courting of preferment, and the wish for vain praise, all of which pass away with the world. Position contributes little if the spirit of fervour is wanting. Nor will that peace last long which is sought on the surface, if the heart's condition has no real grounding. This means that unless you stand immoveably in me, you can have change but not betterment. For when the opportunity arises and is taken, you meet with what you shunned, and more.

Prayer for a clean heart and heavenly wisdom

Strengthen me O God by the grace of the holy spirit. Give me power to grow stronger in the inner man, and to empty my heart of every useless anxiety and distress: not to be carried about by different desires of any thing whether worthless or prized, but to look on all things as passing away, and I too passing with them, since nothing under the sun is lasting, here where all is vanity and vexation of spirit. O how wise is he who thus looks upon them.

O Lord give me heavenly wisdom that beyond all things I may learn to seek and find thee, to taste and love thee above all, and to understand the rest to be the ordering of thy wisdom, as indeed they are.

Give me discretion to escape the flatterer, and patience to endure opposition: for this is great wisdom, not to be moved by every wind of words, nor to give ear to the falsely flattering siren: for the way so begun will be pursued in safety.

28. Against the tongues of slanderers

SON, TAKE it not amiss if some think ill of you and say things you would rather not hear. You should think worse of yourself, and believe that none are weaker than you. If you walk from within, you will not think much of flying words. It is no little discretion to be silent in an evil hour, and to turn inwardly to me, untroubled by human opinion.

Your peace does not depend on the tongues of men. For whether they infer well or ill of you, you still remain the same man. Where is true peace, true glory? In me, surely? And he who neither makes for pleasing men, nor is afraid of displeasing them, will enjoy a goodly measure of peace. All restlessness of heart and distraction of thoughts spring from unrestrained affection and needless fear.

29. How in the moment of trial God should be invoked and blessed

THY NAME O Lord be blessed for ever, for thou hast willed this trial to come upon me. I cannot escape it, but must needs fly to thee that thou mayst help me, and turn it into good for me.

Now am I troubled Lord, and it is not well with my heart: I am sore afflicted by this moment's suffering. And now, beloved Father, what can I say? I am caught in straits. Save me from this hour. Yet for this have I come to this hour, that thou shouldst be made plain to me when I shall be thoroughly humbled and then set free by thee. May it please thee Lord to bring me out: for, poor me, what can I do, and where go without thee? O Lord give me patience even in this misfortune. Help me my God, and I shall not be afraid however much I be oppressed.

And now in the midst of these what shall I say? Thy will be done, O Lord: I well deserve to be troubled and weighed down. I must certainly bear up, and may it be with patience, till the storm blows over and brings a better day. Yet even this trial thine all-powerful hand can lift from me, and lessen its force, lest I utterly succumb: as thou so many times hast done for me before. And the harder it is for me, the easier for thee this turning of the right hand of the Most High.

30. Of asking for divine help, and confidence of again receiving grace

SON, I am the Lord, giving strength in the hour of trouble. Come to me when things have not gone well with you. That which most hinders heavenly comfort is that you are so slow in turning to prayer. For before you ask me intently, you first look round towards many a comfort, and would refresh yourself by external means. So it comes about that all is of little good till you realise that I am he who rescues those who trust in me, and there is no strong aid apart from me, nor sane judgment, nor permanent cure.

But now, taking breath again after the storm, regain your strength in the gleam of my compassion, for I am at hand, says the Lord, to restore everyone, not only with entirety but with abundance, and more too. Can anything be difficult to me, or shall I be as one who says but does not? Where is your faith? Stand firmly and perseveringly. Be a man of patience and courage: comfort will come to you in due time. Wait for me, wait: I will come and heal you.

It is temptation that harasses you, and empty fear that terrorises you. What does anxiety about future events bring but melancholy after melancholy? Its own evil is enough for one day. It is idle and useless to be perturbed or excited about future things that may perhaps never happen. But it is human to be played with by fancies such as these, and the sign of a mind still weak, to be so easily led by a suggestion of the enemy. For he cares not whether he mocks and deceives you by the true or the false: whether he subverts you by love of the present or dread of the future. Therefore let not your heart be troubled or afraid. Trust in me, and be assured of my compassion.

When you think yourself far from me I am often closest to you. When you are considering everything well-nigh lost, often the prize of highest worth awaits you just then.

All is not lost when a thing turns out contrary. You should not judge by the feeling of the moment, nor take up and dwell upon any hardship whencesoever it may come: as if all hope of getting clear had been taken away. Do not think yourself totally bereft, although for the time being I may have sent you some tribulation, or even taken away some pleasant comfort. For so the kingdom of heaven is reached. And without doubt this being drilled in adversities helps you and the rest of my servants more than having everything you wish.

I have known your secret thoughts, and that it is better for your well-being to be left without taste at times lest perhaps you become too conceited with good fortune, and feel pleased with yourself in something you really are not. What I gave I can take away, and restore when I choose. When I give, it is my own: when I take away, I do not take what is yours, for every good gift is mine, and every perfect gift. If I send you something hard or contrary, do not chafe nor break your heart: I can soon uplift and change every burden into a joy. As I have said: I am just, and the more to be trusted in thus dealing with you. If you rightly understand and face the truth, you should never be so abjectly sad over adversities, but even be glad, and give thanks, yes, consider this a peculiar joy that in striking you with sorrows I do not spare you. As the Father loved me, so I love you, I said to my disciples, those whom I certainly did not send out for the delights of time but for hard struggles, not for honours but for scorn, not for ease but toil, not for rest but through suffering to bear plenteous fruit. Be mindful of these words, my son.

31. Of passing by all that is created so as to find the creator

LORD, I still need a larger grace if I am to make my way to that point where neither man nor any other creation can detain me. For while anything holds me fast I am not free to fly to thee. He longed to fly freely who said: "Who will give me wings like a dove's for me to fly away and rest?" What is more at rest than the guileless eye? And who more free than one who desires nothing on earth? One ought at last to rise beyond every created thing and leave self completely behind, and stand in mental ecstasy gazing on thee, the maker of all, who has nothing in creation like thyself. And unless one were set free from all created things one could not be freely intent upon divine things.

That is why so few men of contemplation are to be found, because few know how to seclude themselves enough from what is made and must perish. A great gift is needed for this: one that can uplift the soul and carry it beyond itself. And unless a man is uplifted in spirit, and set free from every creature, and made completely at one with God: whatever he knows, and whatever he has, is of little weight. Long will he be small, and lie in the depths, who accounts as great aught but the one only measureless unending good. And whatever is not God is nothing, and should be thought of as nothing.

There is vast difference between the wisdom of an illumined and devout man, and the knowledge of a well-read and studious cleric. Far more excellent is that teaching which distils from above out of the divine stream, than that acquired by human intellect.

Many are found eager for the contemplative life, but they do not try to practise what is necessary for it. One great hindrance is that they rely on symbols and feelings, and care little about thoroughly killing out self. I do not know what it is, by what impulse we are led, or what we, who are thought and spoken of as spiritual, really mean when we spend so much toil and over-much anxiety on transitory and petty affairs, and seldom scarce think of our inward life with a fully attentive mind. What a pity that after a short recollection we instantly break away without examining our actions with a strict scrutiny. We do not notice where we place our affections, nor regret how impure they all are. It was because all flesh had corrupted its way that the great deluge followed. So when our inward affection is very corrupt, it must needs be that the ensuing act, sign of weakened vigour within, must also be corrupt.

Out of a clean heart comes the fruit of a good life. We ask how much a man has done, but by what determined goodness he does it is not so carefully considered. We ask whether he was brave, rich, handsome, capable, or a good writer, a good singer, or a good workman: but as to how poor in spirit he was, how patient and meek, how devout and inward, we are mostly silent. Nature looks on the outward things of a man, grace turns itself towards the inner. The one is often misled, the other trusts in God and is not deceived.

32. Of self-denial and renunciation of all covetousness

SON, YOU cannot have perfect freedom unless you entirely give up self. Lovers of ownership and self are all fettered, wandering wheels of desire and adventure, always searching for smooth ways, not those of Jesus Christ: generally planning and raising that which will not last. For all will vanish which does not take its rise from God. Hold fast the short and consummate proverb: "lose all and you find all, cease quest and you find rest". Turn this over in your mind, and when content with it you will comprehend all.

Lord, this is no one day's work, nor child's play: indeed in this brief word is set all the perfection of the religious.

Son, you should not be discouraged nor cast down immediately on hearing about the way of perfection, but be spurred the more to greater heights, or at least pant with longing for them. Would you were like this, and had reached the point when you were no lover of self, but would

stand humbly at my beck, and his whom I made a father to
you: then would you surely please me, and all your life
would pass in joy and peace.

You have still much to give up, and unless you surrender
whole-heartedly you will not get what you ask. I advise you
to buy from me gold tried in the fire, that you may become
rich, that is, heavenly wisdom, which treads under foot all
that is base. Think less of earthly wisdom, all pleasing of
man and self. I have said, get for yourself things less prized
in human affairs instead of those precious and highly
esteemed, for true heavenly wisdom seems very poor and
small and almost ignored because it does not think highly
of itself nor seek to be made much of on earth, and so, many
preach it by mouth though in their life they are far from it,
and yet though concealed from the multitude, it is in itself
a priceless pearl.

33. Of the heart's fickleness and of keeping our ultimate intention God-ward

SON, TRUST not your mood of the moment: it will quickly
be changed to some other. As long as you live you are
prone to change even against your will, so that at one time
you find yourself happy, at another sad, at one time calm, at
another restless; now devout, then without devotion; now
studious, then aimless; now grave, then trivial.

But the wise and well trained in spirit is set above these
things, not being keen about what he feels, or from what
quarter the unsettling wind blows, but only that his entire
mental purpose shall make for the right and wished-for end.
For so he will be able to remain unshaken, one and the same,
with the single eye of a purpose fixed direct on me amid
such varied happenings. But the purer the eye's intention
is, the more steadily he presses on through the changing
gusts. But the eye of pure intention is dimmed for many,
because it so quickly looks away to any pleasant thing that

meets it, for it is rare to find anyone quite free of the birth-mark of self-seeking. Thus the Jews of old came to Martha and Mary in Bethany, not so much because of Jesus, as to see Lazarus. Therefore the eye of settled purpose must be cleansed so that it may be single and straight-forward, and beyond all the various things that come between, be kept turned towards me.

34. *That to one who loves him God is enjoyed above all and in all*

Lo, MY God and my all. What more do I wish, and what happier thing can I desire? O sweet and relished word, to one who loves the Word indeed, not the world nor worldly things. My God and my all. That says enough to one who understands: yes, and to the loving heart it is a joy to repeat time after time. For with thee at hand all things are delightful, but with thee absent all is distasteful. Thou givest a tranquil heart and great peace with festive gladness. Thou makest one think kindly of all and praise thee for everything, nor can anything satisfy for long without thee, for if it is to be pleasing and sweet, thy grace must be there, seasoned with the spice of thy deep wisdom. To whom thou art sweet savour, what will not be truly sweet? And to him who has no taste for thee, what can there be for him to enjoy? But the knowing ones of the world, and those who revel in the flesh, fall short of thy discerning light, and so the one finds many an unreal truth, and the other death.

Yet they who instinctively come to thee through disregard of the earthly, being as if dead to the flesh, are known to be truly wise because they are carried on from unreality to truth, from flesh to spirit. God tastes sweet to them, and whatever good is found in creation they turn entirely into praise of its maker. Yet unlike and most unlike is the savour of maker and made, of eternity and time, of light uncreated and the lamp that is lit.

O light perpetual, transcending all created lights, shine with thy brightness from above, piercing all my inmost heart. Make my spirit and all its powers pure, glad, clear, and alert, clinging fast to thee in excess of joy.

Oh, when will it come, that blessed and desirable hour when thy presence will fill me, and thou be all in all to me. Till this be given, joy will not be complete. Still alas the old man lives in me: not wholly crucified is he, not truly dead: still does he fiercely lust against the spirit, stirs inward wars, lets not the soul's realm be quieted. But thou who rulest the ocean's might and calmest the rolling waves, arise and help me. Scatter the brood that wish for war, quell them with thy might, show thy great deeds I pray, and let thy right hand be made glorious: for there is no other hope or refuge for me but in thee, O Lord my God.

35. *That in this life there is no security against temptation*

Son, you are never safe in this life, but as long as you live you will always need spiritual arms. You are in the midst of foes, and are attacked right and left. If you do not use the shield of endurance on every side you will not be long without a wound. Then too, if you do not set your heart immovably upon me, with a plain determination to do everything for me, then you will not be able to keep up this strenuous fight, nor gain the palm of the blessed. You must therefore go through it all like a man, and use a strong hand against the opposing force. For manna is given to him who carries the day, and many an ill remains for him who is slack.

If you search after rest in this life, how then will you come through to an everlasting rest? Do not set out for much in the way of rest, but for suffering that costs. Seek not true peace on earth, but in heaven: neither in men nor in other creatures, but in God only. For love of God you should undergo everything cheerfully: for example, toils and pains, trials, vexations, anxieties, wants, sickness, wrongs, contradictions, reproofs, humiliations, distresses, corrections, and contempt. These are aids to character: these test the soldier of Christ: these shape the heavenly crown. I will give unending pay for short service, and measureless honour for transitory distress.

Do you think you will always have spiritual encouragement at your will? My saints did not have such a thing always, but many burdens and varied trials, and hours of great loneliness. But they bore up patiently through all, and relied on God more than on themselves, knowing that the sufferings of this present time are not worthy to be compared with the glory that is to be. Would you expect to have straightaway what many hardly obtained after many tears and great efforts? Await the Master, act like a man, and be brave: despair not nor give up, but with constancy offer body and soul for the glory of God. I will plenteously repay: I will be with you throughout every tribulation.

36. *Against the groundless judgments of men*

SON, CAST your heart firmly on the Lord, and you will fear no human judgment when conscience declares you upright and innocent. It is good and blessed to suffer in that way: it will not be hard to the lowly of heart, and to one who relies more on God than on himself.

Many talk a great deal, and for that reason little faith is placed in them. In fact it is impossible to satisfy everyone. Though Paul tried to please all in the Lord, and made himself all things to all men, yet he considered it a very small matter to be tried by human judgment. He did enough, as much as was in him to do, for the uplifting and saving of others, yet he could not prevent himself being judged and scorned at times by others. So he left it all with God who knew all, and patiently and humbly defended himself against the unfair tongues of talkers, and whatever words they chose to throw at him, or even their idle and lying thoughts. But now and then he returned like for like lest by his silence a wrong impression might arise in weak brethren.

Who are you that you should be timid before mortal man? Today he is, and tomorrow is not to be seen. Fear God, and you will not dread the terrors of men. What can any man do to you by words or injuries? He hurts himself more than you, and he cannot escape God's judgment, whoever he is. Keep God before your eyes and do not argue against querulous words. And if at the moment you seem to be worsted, and to suffer an undeserved disgrace, do not be indignant at this, nor spoil your crown by impatience, but look the more to me in heaven, for I can lift you out from every shame and wrong, and give back to each one according to his deeds.

37. *Of pure and complete resignation of self for gaining inward freedom*

Son, give up self and you will find me. Stay at your post without a preference or any sense of possession, and you will always be the gainer. For yet fuller grace will be added to you the moment you resign self and do not resume it.

Lord, how often shall I resign myself, and in what ways give up self?

Always and every hour, in small things as in great. I make no exception, but wish to find you stripped of everything. Else how can you be mine and I yours, unless you be spoiled of all self-will within and without? The sooner you do this the better it will be for you; and the more completely and genuinely done the more will you please me, and the fuller will be your gain. Some resign self, but with certain reservation, for they do not trust God entirely, so try to safeguard their own future. Some, too, offer everything at first, but afterwards, beaten by temptations, they go back again to their own, so making hardly any advance towards excellence. These will not attain the real freedom of the pure heart and the influence of joyous intimacy with me, unless they first make a daily offering of self, with absolute resignation, without which the joyful union is neither begun nor can continue.

I have very often said to you, and now I say again, abandon self, give up self, and you will have the joy of great inward peace. Give all for all, ask for nothing, claim nothing back: stand purely and unhesitatingly with me, and you will possess me. You will be free in heart, and gloom will not oppress you. Strive for this, pray for this, long for this: that you may be spoiled of every possession, and being destitute follow the destitute Jesus, as dead to self, and living eternally to me. Then will all idle fancies, false disquietudes, and needless cares fall away. Then, too, unbridled fear will ebb away, and unruly passion die.

38. Of ruling oneself well in outward things and of hastening to God in dangers

SON, YOU should aim earnestly at this, that in every matter and outward action or business you may be inwardly free and master of yourself: so that all things may be under you, and not you under them: that you may be lord and ruler of your actions, not a slave nor a hireling, but rather a free and true Hebrew going on to the destiny and freedom of sons of God who stand upon the present and look towards the eternal: with the left eye seeing the transitory and with the right the heavenly: whom things of time draw not to dwell upon, but are themselves drawn to better service: as they were meant by God to be, and planned by the prime maker, who left nothing purposeless in his creation.

If too in every issue you do not stop at the outward seeming, nor with a bodily eye wander over the seen and heard, but in any case soon enter into the tabernacle with Moses to confer with the Lord, you will sometimes hear the divine reply, and return well-versed in many things present and future. For Moses always had recourse to the tabernacle for the solving of doubts and questions, and flew to the help of prayer for support amid dangers and the wickedness of men. So too should you take refuge in the secret chamber of your heart, entreating earnestly the divine help. For we read that Joshua and the sons of Israel were deceived by the Gibeonites because of this, that they did not first ask from the mouth of the Lord, but, too trustful of soft words, were deluded by pretended loyalty.

39. That a man should not be too keen in business matters

Son, ALWAYS entrust your business to me: I will set it in good order in its own time. Await my arranging of it, and you will see the gain in that.

Lord, cheerfully enough I give over everything to thee, for little can my judgment help. Would that I cared less about things of the future, but unhesitatingly gave myself up to pleasing thee. Son, a man is often fiercely urged towards a certain thing he wants, but when he gets it he begins to feel differently, because the liking for the same thing does not last, but drives him instead from one thing to another. So that it is no slight matter to give up self even in the smallest things. Denial of self is the true advance of a man. And the self-denying man is assuredly free and safe. But the old enemy, being all against good, does not cease from tempting, but by day and night sets strong snares to draw the unwary, by any means he can, into the artful trap. Watch and pray, the Lord says, that you enter not into temptation.

40. That a man has nothing good through him-self and can boast of nothing

LORD, WHAT is man that thou art mindful of him, or a son of man that thou visitest him? How has man deserved to be given thy favour? Lord, how can I complain if thou leave me, or how can I rightly protest if thou do not what I ask? Surely this I may truly think and say: Lord, nothing am I, nothing can I, nothing good have I of myself, but I fail in everything and tend towards nothing. Unless I be helped, and moulded inwardly by thee, I become utterly languid and lax. But thou Lord art ever thy same self, and through eternity continuest always good, just, and holy, doing all things well, justly, and in holiness, and disposing them with wisdom: whilst I, who am readier to fall back than to press on, cannot always hold out in one mood, because seven run through me.

Nevertheless it soon becomes better for me when thou pleasest to hold out a helping hand, for thou alone, without human aid, canst so help and strengthen, that my face shall no more be turned to various things, but to thee alone will my heart be turned and at rest.

So if I could put aside thoroughly all human consolation, either to attain devoutness or because of the necessity which drives me to seek thee, since no man can comfort me, then I might deservedly hope for thy grace, and exult in the giving of a comfort as yet unknown.

Thanks to thee from whom comes all that goes well for me. Yet am I void and naught before thee: a man changeable and weak. Of what then can I boast, or why wish to be thought much of? Can something come out of nothing? So this is the chief vanity.

Truly, empty glorying is an evil pest, the greatest of vanities, since it draws one away from true glory, and steals the grace of heaven. For while a man pleases himself he displeases thee: while he gapes after human praises he loses the real virtues. But true glory and holy exultation is to glory in thee and not in self, to find joy in thy name, nor to delight in anything made, except because of thee.

Thy name be praised, not mine: thy work made much of, not mine: thy holy name be blessed, but none of men's praises be given to me. Thou my glory, thou the exultation of my heart, in thee will I glory and rejoice the whole day long: but for myself no glorying save in my weaknesses. Jews may seek glory from each other: I ask that which is from God alone. Compared with thine eternal glory, all human glory whatsoever, all temporal honours, all earthly loftiness is vanity and folly. O my truth, my mercy, and my God, blessed Trinity, to thee alone be praise, honour, power, glory, through the unending ages.

41. *Of indifference towards every temporal honour*

SON, DO not shrink into yourself if you see others honoured and raised aloft, but you yourself looked down on and brought low. Lift up your heart to me in heaven, and the contempt of men on earth will not grieve you.

Lord, we are in a blind state, and quickly misled by vanity. If I properly examine myself, no creature has ever done me an injustice for which I could honestly complain against thee. But because I have often and gravely sinned against thee I deserve that all creatures should be in arms against me. Distress and contempt are therefore justly due to me, but praise, honour and glory to thee. And unless I prepare myself for this, and be cheerfully ready to be scorned and deserted by every creature, and regarded as altogether nothing, I cannot be inwardly at peace and steadfast, nor spiritually illumined nor fully united to thee.

42. *That peace must not depend on men*

SON, IF you make your peace depend on any person as akin to you in feeling and companionship, you will be unsettled and entangled. But if you have recourse to the ever-living and abiding truth, the separating from or the death of a friend will not overwhelm you. The love of a friend should be rooted in me, and he is to be loved through me whoever seems to you good and very dear in this life. Without me friendship is neither strong nor lasting, nor is that a true and pure love which I do not bind.

You should be so dead to that kind of feeling from men drawn to you that, so far as affects yourself, you would prefer to do without all human comradeship. Man draws so much the nearer to God, the farther he removes from every earthly solace. The higher, too, he rises towards God, the deeper he penetrates self and deems himself more worthless. But he who attributes any good to himself hinders the grace of God from coming into him. If you knew how to annihilate self completely, and be empty of all created love, then should I be diffused through thee with profound effect. When you turn to look at the created the sight of the Creator is withdrawn from you. Learn to conquer self in everything for the Creator's sake: then you will be able to come to divine knowledge. If you excessively dwell on and love anything, however insignificant it be, it keeps you back from what is highest and mars you.

43. *Against conceited and worldly knowledge*

SON, DO not let the charming and cunning assertions of men drive you. For the kingdom of God is not in word, but in power. Await my words which kindle hearts and illumine minds, induce penitence and implant varied consolation. Never read a word just to seem more scholarly or wise.

Take pains to kill out vices, because this will be more useful to you than the conning of many hard problems. When you have read and come to know many things, you always have to revert to the one source.

I am he who teaches man knowledge, and I give clearer understanding to little ones than can be taught by man. He to whom I speak will swiftly be wise and will go far in spirit. Woe to those who search into many a curious quest as to men, and care little about the way of serving me. A time will come when the master of masters, Christ the head-master of angels, will appear to hear the lessons of all: that is, to examine the secret knowledge of each one: and then he will search Jerusalem with lamps, and things hidden in the dark shall be brought to light, and the arguments of tongues shall be stilled.

I am he who in a moment raises the lowly mind to take in more reasons for eternal truth than if one had studied ten years in the schools. I teach without din of words, without confusion of opinions, without arrogance of office, without battling of arguments. I am he who teaches how to look down on the earthly, to be dissatisfied with the present, to seek the everlasting, to taste the eternal, to shun honours, to bear up against scandal, to rest every hope on me, to desire nothing beyond me, and above all, to love me ardently.

For a certain one loving me from his heart, learned divine things, and told of them wonderfully. In giving up all he gained more than by studying fine distinctions. But to some I speak of what is plain to all; to others, words of special meaning: I appear gradually to some in signs and dim forms, but to others indeed I unveil mysteries in the fulness of light. The language of books is one, but it does not teach all equally: for, within, I am teacher, truth, scrutineer of the heart, reader of the thoughts, helper of deeds, dividing to each as I judge fit.

44. *Of not being drawn away to things outside ourselves*

SON, YOU should remain ignorant as to many matters, and consider yourself dead to earth, one to whom everything earthly is crucified. With a deaf ear you must let much go by, and meditate rather on those which make for your peace. It is better to turn your eyes away from things that only annoy, and leave each one to think for himself, rather than be enslaved by wordy arguments. If you stand well with God, and keep his judgment in sight, you will the easier bear up against defeat.

O Lord, to what have we come? See how we bemoan a temporal loss: for a petty gain we toil and rush: and the spiritual gain passes into the forgotten, and is with difficulty returned to at last. We seek after what is of little or no good, and carelessly pass by what is of first necessity: because man as a whole descends to externals, and, unless he quickly draws back, settles down cheerfully among things outside himself.

45. *That we should not trust everyone, and how easy it is to slip in words*

O LORD, give me help out of trouble, for man's help is vain. How often I have found no loyalty just where I felt certain to have it. So, one's trust in men is hollow, but the safety of the upright is in thee O God.

Blessed be thou, O Lord my God, in all that happens to us. We are weak and unsteady, we easily slip and alter our course. What man can so warily and circumspectly guard himself on every side as not sometime to come to deceit or uncertainty? But he who trusts in thee, O Lord, and strives with a guileless heart, does not so lightly give way. And if he falls into any trouble, however much he may be involved he will soon be brought out by thee, or comforted by thee: for, even to the end, thou wilt not leave one who hopes in thee. Rare is the faithful friend, keeping true through all his friend's misfortunes. Thou, O Lord, thou alone art the most faithful of all, and there is none else like thee.

O how truly wise that holy soul who said: "my mind is firmly settled and grounded in Christ". If it were so with me, the fear of man would not so easily disturb me, nor the arrows of words torment. Who can foresee everything, who can guard against evils ahead? If the foreseen so often hurts, how can the unforeseen do other than wound severely? But, unhappy me, why did I not look better ahead?

Why, too, so lightly trust in others? We are but men, naught else but frail men are we, though many think of and call us angels. In whom shall I trust O Lord? In whom but thee? Thou art the truth which neither deceives nor can be deceived. And, on the other hand, every man may be a liar, weak, unsettled, and very slippery in words, so that one can hardly believe immediately what seems to sound right on the face of it. How carefully hast thou warned us to be on our guard against men, and that a man's foes may be those of his own household, and not to believe if anyone should say, lo, here, lo, there.

I am taught by what I lose, and may it be for my deeper caution and not for foolishness. Be wary, says one, be wary; keep what I say to yourself. And while I keep silence, and believe the thing secret, he himself cannot keep silent about what he asked me to keep, and before long betrays me and himself, and goes off.

Protect me Lord from such stories and dangerous men, for fear I fall into their hands, or do such things myself. Set in my mouth the word that is true and straight, and put the cunning tongue far from me. What I myself would not suffer I ought in every way to avoid doing.

O how good and peace-making to be silent about others: not to believe indiscriminately all that is said, nor carelessly spread it abroad: to unveil oneself to few: to look always to thee, thou seer of the heart: not to be carried round with every wind of words, but to wish that all inward and outward things may be done according to the pleasure of thy will. What a safe way it is for the retaining of heavenly grace, to avoid human show, and not to want what seems to win praise from the outer world, but to follow sedulously all those things which gives zest and betterment to life. How many have been injured by having their virtue recognised and praised too soon: how well grace serves when heeded in silence throughout this frail life which is said to be one entire test and warfare.

46. Of retaining trust in God when words are aimed like darts

SON, STAND fast and rely on me. For what are words but words? They fly through the air but do not hurt a stone. If you are at fault, consider how readily you will correct yourself. If you are aware of nothing against you, think how willingly you endure this for God. It is little enough that at least sometimes you should put up with words, when you cannot yet stand hard knocks.

And why should such little things go right to your heart, unless you are still carnal, and pay more heed to men than you should? For, since you are afraid of being looked down on, you do not want to be censured for faults, and seek a shady bower of excuses. But look deeper into yourself, and you will perceive that earth lives in you still, and the hollow longing to please men. For when you shrink from being abased and disconcerted by failings, it is certainly clear that you are not truly humble, nor dead to the world, nor the world crucified to you. But listen to my word, and you will not heed ten thousand words from men.

Look, if all the things were said against you which could be most maliciously conceived, how could they hurt you if you let them pass over you absolutely, not counting them as more than a straw? Could they take even one hair from you? Yet he who keeps not the heart within, nor God before his eyes, is easily stirred by a word of blame. But he who relies on me, and does not try to stand upon his own judgment, will live without fear of men. For I am the judge and knower of all hidden things: I understand a matter as it took place: I knew the wrong-doer and the one who suffered. That particular word went out through me: this happened with my consent: so that the thoughts of many hearts might be made plain. I will judge the guilty and the innocent: but I chose to test them both first by a secret trial.

Human evidence oft misleads: my decision is true: it will stand and not be overturned. It lies hidden mostly, and is clear, in points, only to the few: but it never errs, nor can err, even if to the eyes of the foolish it may not seem right.

To me therefore must you turn for every decision, not depending on your own authority. For the upright man will not be perplexed whatever happens to him from God. Even if anything unjust is charged against him, he will not trouble much. Neither will he rejoice conceitedly if he be reasonably absolved by others. For he considers how that I am the searcher of the heart and inner man who judges not by the face of things and by human seeming. For often in my eyes that is found blameable which in men's judgment is considered laudable.

O Lord God, righteous judge, strong and patient, who knowest the frailty and perversity of men, be my strength and my whole trust, for my knowledge is not enough for me. Thou knowest what I know not, and therefore in every reproof I ought to humble myself and bear it meekly. When I have not done so, mercifully forgive me, and once more grant me the power of greater endurance. For thy full mercy is better for me in the obtaining of pardon than my imagined righteousness of a hidden conscience used as a defence. Even if I know nothing against myself, yet I cannot by this justify myself, for, with thy mercy withdrawn, no living man will be righteous in thy sight.

47. That for the sake of eternal life all burdens are to be borne

SON, THE toils which you took up for me will not break you, nor will troubles always cast you down, but my promise will strengthen and console you in every event. I can repay you beyond all limit and measure. Not for long will you labour here, nor be depressed with sorrows for ever. Wait a little, and you will see the swift end of evils. An hour will come when all toil and tumult will cease. Scant and brief is all that passes with time.

Do what you are doing: loyally work in my vineyard: I will be your wage. Write, read, sing, mourn, be silent, pray: bear crosses manfully; life eternal is worth all these battles, and greater. Peace will come in a day that is known to the Master, and it will not be the day or night of the age that is, but an everlasting light, an unlimited brightness, a settled peace and safe rest. Not then will you say, who will deliver me from the body of this death: nor cry out, woe is me that my stay is prolonged: for death will be cast headlong down, and health will be unfailing, anxiety unknown, joy a blessedness, fellowship sweet and beautiful.

Oh if you could see the eternal crowns of the saints in heaven, and with what rapture they now exult, who for this world were once deemed contemptible and unfit for life itself, you would surely humble yourself to the dust, and try more to be under all than over even one: nor would you wish for happy days of this life, but rather rejoice in suffering for God, and reckon it greatest gain to be accounted nothing among men.

Oh if you had experienced these things, and they had entered deeply into your heart, how could you complain even once? Are not all laborious pains to be endured as with life eternal in view? It is no slight thing that,—to lose or gain the realm of God. So, lift your face to heaven: behold I, and all my saints with me, they who in this world had great conflict. Now they rejoice, now are they consoled, now are they safe, now have they rest, and for ever will they dwell with me in my Father's kingdom.

48. About the day of eternity and the straits of this life

O MOST blessed dwelling of the supernal city. O brightest day of eternity which no night darkens, but perfect truth always irradiates: a day ever joyous, ever free from care, and never changing to an opposite. O would that day would dawn, and all these things of time be at an end. It shines indeed to saints in splendour of unceasing brightness, but to pilgrims on earth as far away and in a mirror. Citizens of heaven know how full of gladness is yonder state: exiled sons of Eve mourn the bitterness and tedium of this.

Few and evil are the present days of time, full of sorrows and straits, when man is stained with many sins, entangled by many passions, restrained by many fears, pulled by many cares, distraught by many questions, tied up in many vanities, set round with many errors, worn down by many efforts, burdened with temptations, weakened by pleasures, tormented by poverty.

O when will these evils end, when shall I be freed from the wretched slavery of my failures? When shall I be mindful Lord of thee alone, when shall I rejoice to the full in thee? When shall I be truly free of every hindrance, untroubled in mind and body? When shall I have firm peace, peace calm and secure, peace within and without, peace steadfast on every side? Good Jesu, when shall I stand beholding thee, when shall I survey the glory of thy kingdom, when wilt thou be all in all to me? O when shall I be with thee in thy realm which thou hast prepared for thy beloved from eternity? Poor and exiled, I am left in the land of a foe, where fights are daily and misfortunes most great.

Cheer my exile, lighten my sorrow, since my whole longing sighs after thee. For all is a burden to me, whatever this world offers as comfort. Thee do I long to enjoy most closely, but cannot reach. I would dwell on the heavenly, but temporal things and passions not yet dead keep me down. In mind I would rise beyond all mere things, but by the flesh I am forced unwillingly beneath them. So, unhappy man, I fight with myself, and become a trouble to myself because the spirit strives upward and the flesh would stay below.

Oh what I suffer inwardly when with the mind I ponder on heavenly things, and, as I am praying, a crowd of carnal things soon rush in. Go not far from me O my God, nor turn away in anger from thy servant. Flash thy lightning and scatter them: shoot thine arrows and throw all the phantasms of the enemy into confusion. Call back my thoughts to thee, make me forget all worldliness, aid me quickly to fling away and despise the evil dreams.

Truth eternal, help me, that no vain thing may excite me: come thou heavenly sweetness, and every impurity will fly before thy face. Forgive me too, and be tender in pity whenever in prayer I think of aught but thee. I truly confess indeed that I am too ready to give way to mind-wandering. For often I am not there where bodily I stand or sit, but rather I am where I am carried away by thoughts. I am there where my thought is. Often is my thought there where is what I love, which readily presents itself to me, as attracting naturally, or pleasing from habit.

Whence thou, the Truth, didst plainly say, For where thy treasure is there is thy heart also. If I love heaven I readily think of the heavenly. If I love the world I rejoice in the world's happiness and am sad in its adversities. If I love the flesh I often imagine things of the flesh. If I love the spirit I delight in thinking about spiritual things. For whatever I love, of these I cheerfully talk and listen, and so bring home to myself likenesses of them. But blessed is that man who for thy sake O Lord gives all things of earth leave to go, who does violence to nature, and with an ardent will crucifies fleshly desires, in order that with serene conscience he may offer pure prayer to thee and, sheltered from all earthliness without and within, he may become worthy to take part with the angelic choirs.

49. *Of the longing for eternal life, and what good things are promised to those who strive*

SON, WHEN you feel the desire for eternal blessedness pouring in upon you, and you pine to leave the tent of the body that you may gaze on my brightness which has no shadow of change, open wide your heart and receive this holy inspiration with utter longing. Give fullest thanks to the supernal goodness which deals so graciously with you, visits in mercy, quickens fervently, uplifts with power lest of your own weight you should sink back to the earthly. For you neither receive this by your own thought or effort, but simply by the condescension of supreme grace and divine consideration so that you may grow in virtues and a larger humility, prepare yourself for struggles to come, cleave to me with whole-hearted affection, and endeavour to serve with a fervent will.

Son, a fire often glows, yet no flame goes up without smoke. So too some men's desires flare up towards the heavenly, and yet they are not free from temptation by carnal feeling. Therefore they do not aim entirely and purely for God's honour in what they so earnestly ask of him. Such, and often, is your desire which you made out to be so insistent. For that which is tainted by one's own gain is not pure and perfect. Do not ask for what is pleasing and profitable for you, but for what is acceptable and honouring to me, for if you rightly decide, you should prefer my ruling as to your desire and all yet to be desired, and follow it.

I have known your longing and have heard your frequent sighs. You wish to have the freedom of the glory of the sons of God now, to enjoy already the eternal home and the heavenly country filled with gladness, but that hour is not yet come, there is still a further period, namely a time of war, a season of toil and testing. You wish to be filled with the supreme good, but you cannot attain this yet. It is I: look for me, says the Lord, till the kingdom of God shall come. Thou art still to be tried on earth, and be disciplined in many ways. Comfort will at times be given you, but full abundance will not be conceded. Be strong then, and resolute alike in action and in suffering what is against your nature.

You must put on the new man, and be changed into another man. You must often do what you would not, and what you would you must put aside. What pleases others shall go through, what pleases you shall not go far. What others say shall be listened to, what you say will be reckoned as nothing. Others will ask and receive, you will ask but not get. Others will be great in the mouth of men, but of you there will be silence. This or that shall be entrusted to others, but you will be judged as useful for nothing. Your nature will sometimes be saddened at this, and it will be a great thing if you bear it quietly.

In these and many such ways the Lord's faithful servant is usually tested as to how far he can deny and break himself in everything. There is hardly anything in which you so need to die to self as in seeing and enduring things that are against your will: most of all when ordered to be done if they appear to you inconsistent and useless. And because, being under rule, you dare not resist the higher power, therefore it seems hard to you to go at another's nod, and to put by all your own opinion.

But think, son, of the fruit of these efforts, the swift end, the exceeding great reward, and you will have no bitterness left, but the strongest comfort for your patience. Since, for this slight measure of will that now you willingly give up, you will have your will for ever in heaven. There indeed you will meet with all you could wish, all that you will be capable of desiring: there at hand will be abundance of all good without the fear of losing it. There shall your will be always one with mine, desiring nothing extraneous or private. There none will resist you, none complain of you, none hinder, none be in your way: but all things desirable will be present at once, and revive all your love and fill right to the uttermost. There will I return glory for insults borne, a robe of praise for sadness, a royal seat for ever instead of the lowest place. There shall the fruit of obedience be seen, the toiling of penitence rejoice, and lowly subjection be gloriously crowned.

But meanwhile bow yourself humbly under the hands of all, nor care who said or ordered this, but mainly be alert for this, that whether a prelate or a junior or an equal request anything of you, or suggest it, you take it all for good, and try to fulfil it with honest intention. One may seek that, another this: one glories in this and another in that, and may be praised a thousand thousand times, but you neither in this nor that, save in valuing self little, and in pleasing and honouring me alone. This is to be your choice: that whether by living or dying God shall always be glorified in you.

50. How a lonely man should place himself in the hands of God

O LORD God, holy Father, be thou now and for ever blessed, because as thou wilt so is it done, and what thou doest is good. May thy servant be glad in thee, not in self, nor in aught else, for thou alone art true joy, thou my hope and my crown, thou my delight and my honour O Lord.

What has thy servant but what he received from thee, and that without his deserving? Thine are all things thou gavest, and that thou hast done. I am poor and amid struggles from my youth up, and my soul is sad at times even to tears whenever it is disquieted within itself by menacing passions. I long for the joy of peace, I beg for the peace of thy sons who in the light of comfort are fed by thee. If thou givest peace, if thou pour holy joy into me, the soul of thy servant will be filled with melody, and be devout in thy praise. But if thou withdraw, as is too often thy way, he will not be able to run the way of thy laws, but rather he will smite his breast and bend his knees because it is not as yesterday or the day before with him, when thy lamp shone above his head, and in the shadow of thy wings he was protected against the inrush of temptations.

O Father righteous and ever to be praised, the hour comes for thy servant to be tried. Father beloved, it is right that in that hour thy servant should suffer something for thee. Father ever to be worshipped the hour comes which from eternity thou knewest should be, when for a brief time thy servant should outwardly give way, though inwardly he would ever live with thee. For a little while he should be held of no account, he should be humbled, and fail in the eyes of men, and be worn out with sufferings and weariness, -that again he may rise with thee in the dawn of a new light, and be made to shine in heaven. O holy Father, so hast thou ordained and so willed, and that which thou hast ordered is already accomplished. For to thy friend this is a favour to suffer and have trouble in the world for love of thee, however often and by whomsoever thou allowest it to happen. Without thy counsel and foresight, and without cause, nothing on earth is done.

It is good for me Lord that I should be brought low, so that I may learn thy rights, and fling away all inward conceits and presumptions. It is a gain to me when shame has covered my face, if only I look to thee for comfort rather than to men. I learned also from this to fear thy mysterious judgment, thou who strikest the upright with the impious, yet not without equity and justice.

Thanks be thine that thou has not been sparing in my evil doings, but hast worn me down with bitter strokes, inflicting sorrows and sending stresses without and within. There is none out of all under heaven who can console me but thou, O Lord my God, celestial healer of souls, who piercest and makest whole, who takest down to lowest depths and bringest back again.

Beloved Father, lo I am in thy hands, I bow myself beneath the rod of correction, smite my back and my neck, that I may bend my crooked way to thy will. Make me an honest and lowly scholar, as thou wert kindly wont to do, so that I may walk always at thy beck. I entrust myself and all mine to thee to be set right: better it is to be reproved here than hereafter. Thou knowest each and every thing, and nothing in human consciousness escapes thee. Before things are done thou knowest their coming, and hast no need that any teach or remind thee of what is happening on earth. Thou knowest what is good for my progress, and how greatly tribulation helps to clean away the rust of sins. Deal with me according to thy good pleasure, and spurn not my sinful life known to none better nor more clearly than to thee alone. Grant me O Lord to know what should be known, to love what should be loved, to praise what pleases thee most highly, to value what seems precious to thee, to revile what is unclean in thy sight.

May I not judge by the seeing of the outward eyes, nor condemn by the hearing of the untrained ears of men, but with true judgment discern between the visible and the spiritual, and above all be ever searching for the will of thy good pleasure. The thoughts of men often mislead in judging, and lovers of the world are deceived in loving only the things seen.

What better then is a man because he is thought more of

by man? The deceiver deludes the deceitful while he flatters, the vain the vain, the blind the blind, the weak the weak, and each is truly the more misleading as he gives hollow praise. For "what anyone is in thine eyes, such is he and no more," says the lowly Saint Francis.

51. *That one must continue with lowly tasks when one fails in those highest*

SON, YOU cannot always remain with an ardent longing for virtues, nor dwell in the higher stage of contemplation, but sometimes you needs must descend to lower things, because of some original taint, and bear the burden of a decaying life, though wearily and against your will. Whilst you carry a mortal body you will feel weariness and heaviness of heart. Therefore in the flesh you have often to sigh over the burden of the flesh in that you cannot stick unendingly to spiritual efforts and divine contemplation.

At such a time it is good for you to turn yourself to lowly and outward doings, and refresh yourself by doing some good act, looking with settled trust for my coming and the heavenly visitation, bearing your exile and mental dryness patiently till I again come to you and release you from all anxieties. For I will make you forget toils and enjoy innermost quiet, I will spread the fields of holy writings before you, so that with heart enlarged you will begin to run the way of my commands, and say, "the sufferings of this present time are not worthy to be compared with the future glory that shall be revealed to us."

52. *That a man should not think himself deserving of comfort but rather as condemned to chastisement*

O LORD I am not worthy of thy consolation, nor of any spiritual visitation. And so thou actest rightly by me whenever thou leavest me helpless and desolate. For though I might shed a sea of tears, still I should not be worthy of thy comforting. I deserve nothing then but to be scourged and punished because deeply and often have I offended thee, and am greatly wanting in many ways. Truly weighed then by reason I am unworthy of the least consolation. But thou, pitying and merciful God, who desirest not thy works to perish, and in order to show the wealth of thy goodness in vessels of mercy, deignest, even beyond all merit of mine, to comfort thy servant in higher than a human way.

What have I done O Lord that thou shouldst give me any heavenly comfort? I recall nothing good that I have done, but always have I been inclined to faults, and slow to correct them. True it is, and I cannot deny it. If I were to say otherwise thou wouldst stand against me, and there would be none to defend me. What have I deserved for my sins but hell and fire eternal? In truth I admit that I deserve every ridicule and contempt, and am not fit to be named as among thy devoted ones. And though reluctantly I hear this, yet, for truth's sake, I lay my sins open to thee, that I may the more easily win thy mercy.

What shall I, guilty and full of confusion, say? My mouth can utter nothing but just this word: "I have sinned O Lord, I have sinned: pity me, forgive me." Spare me a while, that I may mourn my sorrow, before I go to a land darkened with the mist of death.

What dost thou so much look for from a guilty and hapless sinner as that he should be ground to dust and humiliate himself for his faults? Hope of pardon is born from true contrition and lowliness of heart: the troubled conscience is reconciled: lost grace is restored: man is saved from wrath to come: and God and the penitent soul meet each other in a holy kiss. Humble contrition for sins is an acceptable offering to thee O Lord, smelling far sweeter to thee than burning incense. This too is the pleasing ointment which thou didst wish to be poured on thy holy feet for thou didst not despise the broken and lowly heart. There is the place of refuge from the angry face of the foe: there whatever contamination caught from any quarter is purified and washed clean away.

53. *That the grace of God does not blend with earthly tastes*

SON, MY grace is precious: it will not bear being mingled with extraneous things, nor with earthly satisfactions. Therefore you must cast aside all hindrances to grace if you would receive its inflowing. Find a hiding-place for yourself: love to dwell alone with yourself: invite no-one's idle talk: but rather pour out devout prayer to God that you may keep a quickened mind and a clear conscience.

Reckon the whole world nothing: put freedom for God before everything external. For you cannot be free for me, and at the same time delight in transitory affairs. You must get right away from those known and loved, and keep your mind apart from every temporal solace. So the blessed apostle Peter entreats that Christ's faithful ones should keep themselves as strangers and pilgrims in this world.

O what confidence will be his in dying who is not held back to earth by desire for anything. But the still weak does not yet understand what it is to have the heart set thus apart from all mere things, nor does the physical man know the freedom of the inward man. Yet if he would be truly spiritual, he must renounce the far as well as the near, and beware of no-one more than himself. If you perfectly master your own self you will easily subjugate the rest. The complete victory is to triumph over oneself. For he who keeps himself under, so that the senses obey reason, and reason, in everything, obeys me, he is veritably victor over self and master of the world.

If you wish to climb this height, you must begin like a man and lay the axe to the root: you must pull up and destroy the excessive hidden tendency to self, and to every personal and material gain. From this vice, that man loves himself too immoderately, depends almost everything which has to be radically overcome. This evil mastered and put down, great peace and tranquillity will follow. But because few strive to be perfectly dead to self, they remain therefore inwoven with self, and cannot therefore rise in spirit beyond themselves. But he who would walk freely with me must kill out all his wicked and disordered feelings, and not cling covetously, with self-centred love, to any created thing.

54. Of the differing impulses of nature and grace

SON, NOTE carefully the stirrings of nature and those of grace, for they impel in most subtle and opposite ways, and can scarcely be distinguished except by a spiritual and inwardly enlightened man. All men indeed seek a good, and allege some kind of good in what they say and do, so that many are misled by an apparent good.

Nature is cunning, and influences many, snaring and deceiving, and always has self for its end: But grace goes openly, turns from every appearance of evil, holds out no false promises, and does everything purely for God in whom, and as the end, it rests.

Nature is unwilling to face death, or be burdened, or overcome, or be beneath others, or freely under a yoke: but grace strains after the deadening of self, resists the sensual, aims at being submissive, sets out facing defeat, is not eager to exercise its own liberty, loves to be held in by discipline, not wishing to rule over any, but always to live, stand, and be under God, and for God's sake is ready to bow humbly before every human creature.

Nature works for its own gain, and looks out for what profit it may gather for itself, but grace thinks not of what may be of use and help to itself, but rather what will be best for the many.

Nature cheerfully accepts honour and reverence, but grace faithfully ascribes all honour and glory to God. Nature fears shame and contempt, but grace rejoices to suffer abuse for the name of Jesus.

Nature loves ease and bodily rest, whilst grace cannot be idle readily embraces toil.

Nature looks for the strange and beautiful, and hates the common and coarse: but grace delights in the plain and humble, does not scorn the rough, nor refuse to wear old rags.

Nature keeps an eye on temporal things, rejoices at earthly gains, is depressed by loss, is irritated by a light word of affront: but grace looks towards the eternal, clings not to the temporal, is not disturbed at the loss of things, nor embittered by harsh words, because its joy and treasure are fixed in heaven where nothing is lost.

Nature is covetous and eagerly takes more than it gives, loves personal and private possessions; but grace is tender and shares, it shuns peculiar rights, is satisfied with few things, deems it more blessed to give than to receive.

Nature turns towards things created, to flesh, vanities, and aimless wanderings: but grace leads towards God and the virtues, puts the created aside, avoids the world, hates fleshly desires, restricts roving moods, blushes to appear in public.

Nature gladly accepts any outward comfort in which the senses may be gratified: but grace seeks comfort in God alone, and beyond all visible things delights in the supreme good.

Nature does everything for personal gain and interest: it can do nothing without pay; but for any kindnesses hopes to get either an equivalent or more, or else praise or good-will, and is keen to have its deeds and gifts highly valued: but grace seeks nothing temporal, and as payment asks no other reward than God alone, nor wishes for more temporal neces ities than may help it to gain things eternal.

Nature rejoices in having many friends and kinsmen, glories in noble rank and birth, smiles on the powerful, fawns on the rich, applauds those like itself: but grace loves even its enemies, and is not puffed up because of a crowd of friends, nor thinks much of standing or birth unless it means a finer virtue; it favours the poor more than the rich, it is more in sympathy with the innocent than the powerful, rejoices with the honest not the false, always encourages the good to aim at better gifts and by virtues become like the Son of God.

Nature soon complains about any want or trouble: grace bears poverty with fortitude.

Nature bends everything towards self, struggles and argues for self: but grace leads all things back to God whence they first emerged, ascribes to itself nothing good, nor arrogantly assumes: does not dispute nor prefer its own opinion to that of others, but in every feeling and thought submits itself to the eternal wisdom and divine judgment.

Nature yearns to know hidden things and to hear news: it wants to be seen abroad, and to test many things by experience: it wants to be known, and to do whatever will draw praise and admiration: but grace does not care to know the novel or curious, for all this springs from the old old decay out of which there can be nothing new or lasting. It teaches us therefore to restrain the senses, to avoid empty self-satisfaction and show, to humbly hide things worthy of praise and wonder, and out of everything and through all knowledge to seek after the fruit of service and the praise and honour of God. It does not wish itself or its doings acclaimed, but would choose that God who out of pure love lavishes all things, should be blessed in his gifts.

This grace is a light beyond nature, and in some way a special gift of God, and the peculiar mark of his chosen, an assurance of eternal welfare that lifts a man out of love of the earthly into love of the heavenly, and from a carnal makes a spiritual being. Therefore the more nature is repressed and subdued so much the more is grace poured in, and by new visitations the inner man remoulded after the image of God.

55. Of nature's corruption and the effective power of divine grace

O LORD my God, who hast created me in thine image and likeness, give me this grace which thou hast shown to be so great and so necessary for my safety, that I may conquer my very evil nature which draws me towards sin and ruin. For I feel in my flesh a law of sin contradicting the law of my mind and leading me in captive obedience to the sensuous in many ways: nor can I resist its moods unless thy most holy grace, ardently poured into my heart, assists me. I need thy grace, and plentiful grace, to overcome nature ever prone to evil from my youth.

For through the first man Adam, fallen and infected with sin, the penalty of this stain came down through all men, so that nature itself, which was fashioned good and upright by thee, stands now to mean the vice and weakness of a spoiled nature because, left to itself, its impulse tends towards evil and the lower things. The little strength that remains is but as a spark hidden in the ashes. This is natural reason itself wrapped in great darkness, still possessing knowledge of the difference between good and evil, true and false, although it may be powerless to carry out all it assents to, and cannot yet possess the full light of truth nor the healthful use of its own emotions.

Hence it is, my God, that I with the inner man delight in thy law, knowing thy command to be good, just, and holy, assuring me too that all evil and sin are to be avoided: but I, in the flesh, serve the law of sin when I obey sensual temptation rather than reason. Hence it is that to will the good is mine, but I do not find how to carry it through. Hence I often lay out many good plans but because grace is lacking to help my weak will I hark back and lose hope through a little opposition. So it comes about that I know the way of perfection, and see clearly enough what I ought to do, but being pressed down by the weight of my own corruption I do not rise to the more perfect things.

O how supremely necessary for me is thy grace, O Lord, to begin anything good, to press on with it, and to complete it: for without that I can do nothing, but with thee I can do everything, grace strengthening me. O true celestial grace, without which we have no deserts of our own, nor any natural gifts that count. No arts, no wealth, no beauty nor fortitude, no wit nor eloquence are of any value with thee without grace. For natural gifts are common to good and bad, but the peculiar gift of the elect is grace or love: sealed with this they are held worthy of eternal life. So outstanding is this grace that neither gift of prophecy, nor working of marvels, nor any height of thought is of any value without it. Indeed neither faith nor hope nor any other virtues are acceptable to thee without love and grace.

O most blessed grace which makest the poor in spirit rich in virtues, and causest one rich in goods to be lowly of heart: come, descend into me, fill me early with thy comfort, lest my soul fail through lassitude and mental dryness. I pray O Lord that I may find grace in thine eyes, for thy grace is enough for me, though I get not those other things that nature longs for. When I am tried and vexed with many tribulations I will fear no evil so long as thy grace is with me. She is my strength, she brings counsel and help. She is stronger than every foe, and wiser than all the wise. Mistress of truth is she, teacher of discipline, light of the heart, solace in hard times, dispeller of sadness, expeller of fear, nurse of devotion, bringer of tears. Without her what am I but a dry tree and a useless branch, fit to be thrown away? Therefore O Lord let thy grace precede and follow me always, and make me continually active in good works, through Jesus Christ thy Son. Amen.

56. That we should deny ourselves and imitate Christ through a cross

SON, THE more you rise beyond self, the more transformed into me can you be. As the coveting of nothing outward makes for inward peace, so the deeper yielding up of self unites you with God. I want you to learn a yet more perfect abnegation of self into my will, without a word against or complaint.

Follow me. I am the way, the truth, and the life. Without the way there is no going, without the truth there is no knowing, without the life there is no living. I am the way which you should follow, the truth which you should trust, the life which you should hope for. I am the way unchangeable, the truth infallible, the life unendable. The straightest way am I, the truth supreme, the real life, life blessed, uncreated life. If you keep in my way you will understand truth, and truth will set you free, and you will attain life eternal. If you would enter into life keep the commandments. If you would understand truth, trust me. If you would be perfect, sell all. If you would be my follower, deny your very self. If you would gain life blessed, think nothing of life present. If you would be set high in heaven, humble yourself on earth. If you would reign with me, carry a cross with me. For only bearers of a cross find the road of blessedness and true light.

O Lord Jesu since thy way was straitened and scorned by the world, let it be mine to imitate thee in the world's contempt, for a servant is not greater than his lord, nor a learner above a master. Train thy servant in thy life, for there lies my welfare and true holiness. Whatever I read or hear outside that neither refreshes nor delights me wholly.

Son, because you know and have read all these things, blessed will you be if you do them. He who knows my words and keeps them, he it is who loves me. And I will love him and reveal my very self to him, and will make him sit beside me in my Father's kingdom.

O Lord Jesus as thou hast spoken and promised, so truly let it be, and be it mine to deserve it. I have taken a cross, I took it from thy hand: I will bear it, yes I will bear it even unto death since thou hast placed it on me. Truly the life of a good monk is a cross, but a guide to paradise. Once begun, one may not go back, nor is it right to give up.

Come brothers, let us go on together, Jesus will be with us. For Jesus we took up this cross, for Jesus let us persevere with the cross. He will be our helper who is our leader and fore-runner. See, before us goes our king who will fight for us. Let us follow manfully, let none shrink at terrors: let us be ready to die bravely in the battle without bringing that disgrace on our glory that we fled from the cross.

57. That a man should not be too cast down when he slips into some faults

SON, PATIENCE and humility in adversities please me more than much satisfaction and devotion in prosperous times. Why let a little thing said against you grieve you so? If it had been greater still, you should not have been disturbed. But now let it go. It is not the first, nor is it a new thing, nor will it be the last if you live long enough. You are manly enough while no opposition is in the way. You can give good advice, and know how to strengthen others by words: but when trouble comes suddenly to your own door you fail in counsel and courage.

Remember your great frailty, which you have often experienced in minor trials. Yet these were meant for your good, when they and their like came on you. Put it out of your heart, because you know better: and if it touches you, still, do not be cast down or entangled for long. Bear it at least patiently if you cannot joyfully. Although you would rather not hear of it, and feel irritated, check yourself, not allowing any sharp word to come from your mouth by which the little ones may be hurt. Your excitement will soon quiet down, and the inward smart be softened by returning grace.

I abide still, says the Lord, ready to help you and give more than common solace if you trust me and call devoutly. Be more quiet, and gird yourself for greater endurance: all is not in vain, though you feel troubled or gravely tempted. You are a man, and not God: you are flesh, not an angel. How can you always remain in the same state of virtue when this was wanting in an angel in heaven and in the first man in paradise? It is I who raise the mourners to safety, and transport into my divinity those who recognise their own frailty.

Blessed be thy word O Lord, sweeter in my mouth than honey and the honeycomb. What should I do amid so many of my troubles and straits, unless thou strengthen me with thy holy words? If only I may reach the port of safety, what shall I care what I suffer and how much? Grant me but a good end, give me a happy passing out of this world. Bear me in mind, O God, and guide me in a straight path to thy kingdom. Amen.

58. Of not peering into the higher concerns and hidden judgments of God

SON, BEWARE of questioning as to the high affairs and secret decisions of God: why this one was so left to himself, and that one received such favour, or why this one was so stricken, and the other so highly exalted. These things are beyond every human faculty of knowing, nor can any reason or argument avail to trace out the course of divine decision.

Therefore when the enemy suggests these questions to you, or again some inquisitive men pry into them, answer like the prophet: "just art thou O Lord, and thy decision is right," and also, "the judgments of the Lord are true, justified in themselves." My judgments are to be feared not discussed, because they are not to be comprehended by the human intellect.

Also, do not search into or dispute about the merits of saints, which is holier than the other, or which will be greater in the kingdom of heaven. Such questions often breed discord and useless contentions, and also nourish pride and vain-glory whence arise envies and dissensions as one proudly tries to put forward this saint, and the other another. But wishing to know and seek into such things bears no fruit, but is rather displeasing to the saints: for I am not the God of dissension but of peace, which peace rests more on true humility than on self-exaltation. Some are attracted by a zealous affection and fuller sympathy to these or to those, but this impulse is more human than divine.

It is I who built up all the saints: I bestowed grace, I set the glory before them. I know the merits of each, I anticipated them with the blessings of my sweetness, I foreknew my beloved ones ere time was. I chose them out of the world, they did not first choose me. I called them by grace, I drew them by pity. I led them through varied temptations, I pervaded with lavish consolations, I bestowed perseverance, I crowned their patience. I know them from first to last, I enfold them all with a measureless love. I am to be praised through all my saints: beyond all am I to be blessed and honoured through each and all of those whom I made so gloriously great, and fore-ordained without any previous merits of their own.

Therefore he who looks down on one of the least of mine honours not the great, for I made small and great. And he who disparages any of the saints, disparages me and all others in the kingdom of heaven. All are one by the bond of charity, feel alike, will alike, and all love as with one being. But still, what is much higher, they love me more than themselves and their own worth. For rapt beyond self, and drawn away from self-love, they pass entirely through into love of me, where they rest in enjoyment. There is nothing that can turn them aside or depress them, for those filled with truth everlasting but with the fire of love unquenchable.

Therefore carnal and earth-bound men, who know not how to love anything save their own personal pleasures, should keep silent, and not discuss the standing of the saints. They take away and add just as they fancy, not as satisfying truth eternal. In many it is simply ignorance, mainly in those who, insufficiently enlightened, know not how to love anyone with a perfectly spiritual love. At the same time they are greatly drawn by natural feeling and human friendship to this one or that, and, as they themselves live on lower levels, so their imagination shapes the heavenly conditions. But there is an incomparable distance between what they imperfectly picture and what enlightened men see by revelation from on high.

Beware therefore, son, of inquisitively handling these things which exceed your knowledge, but rather try and aim at this, that, even if least, you may be found in the kingdom of God. Even if any man were to know who is holier or held greater than another in the kingdom of heaven, what would he gain by this knowing, unless because of that knowledge he should humble himself before me, and be moved to greater praise of my name? He who realises the magnitude of his sins and the fewness of his virtues, and how far he stands from the perfection of the saints, becomes much more acceptable to God than he who argues as to the greater or lesser status of the saints.

It is better to call on the saints with devout prayers and tears, and with lowly mind implore their glorious aid, than to press with useless questioning into their veiled mysteries. They are well, full well contented if men would but know how to contain and curb their idle talk. They do not glory in their own deservings, for they ascribe nothing good to themselves, but the whole of it to me, because I gave them everything out of my infinite love. They are filled with so great a love of the divine, and such overflowing joy, that for them no glory is wanting, and no felicity can be lacking. The more exalted all the saints are in glory, so the lowlier they are in themselves, and the nearer and dearer to me. So you have it written that they cast down their crowns before God and fell on their faces before the Lamb, and worshipped him who lives for ever and ever.

Many try to find who is greater in God's kingdom, themselves not knowing whether they will deserve to be counted even among the least. It is a great thing to be even least in heaven, where all are great because all will be called and be sons of God. The least shall be as a thousand, and the sinner a hundred years old shall die. For when the disciples asked who would be greatest in the kingdom of heaven, this was the answer they heard: "except ye be converted and become as little children ye shall not enter into the kingdom of heaven. Whosoever therefore shall humble himself as this little child, this same is the greater in the kingdom of heaven."

Woe to those who disdain to humble themselves willingly with the little ones, for the lowly gate of the celestial kingdom will not let them enter in. Woe also to the rich who have their comforts here, for while the poor are entering the kingdom of God, they themselves will stand outside lamenting. Rejoice ye humble, and exult ye poor, for the kingdom of God is yours if ye keep the true way in spite of all.

59. That all hope and trust should be fixed on God alone

O LORD, what trust is there for me to hold throughout this life, or what my greatest comfort out of all that is to be seen under heaven? Is it not thyself O Lord my God, of whose tenderness there is no limit? When was it ever well with me without thee? Or when could it ever be ill, with thee at hand? I would rather be poor for thy sake, than rich without thee. I would rather choose to be a wanderer over the earth with thee, than possess heaven without thee. Where thou art, there it is heaven: and where thou art not, there it is death and the underworld. Thou art my desire, and therefore must I sigh for thee, cry out and pray.

In none at last can I fully trust for timely help in moments of necessity save in thee alone, my God. Thou art my hope, thou my assurance, thou my comforter and most to be relied on in all ways. All seek their own ends: thou alone dost intend my welfare and my progress, and turnest everything to good for me. Even if thou leavest me open to trials and adversities, this thou, who in a thousand ways art wont to test thy loved ones, orderest entirely for my good. In which testing of me thou shouldst be no less loved and praised than if thou hadst filled me with heavenly consolations.

In thee therefore O Lord my God I place my entire hope and refuge, before thee I lay down all my trouble and stress, for whatever I look to outside thee I find feeble and unsettled. For one's many friends avail not, nor can strong helpers aid, nor careful advisers give sound opinion, nor books of the learned console, nor any precious substance set me free, nor any secret pleasant place safeguard, if thou thyself dost not stand by, help, strengthen, comfort, teach, and guard. For all the things that seem to promise peace and happiness are nothing without thee, and bring in truth no happiness. Thou therefore art the final cause of every good, the height of life, the depth of utterance, and to rely on thee is the most powerful comfort of thy servants. To thee my eyes are turned: in thee, my God, I trust, father of mercies.

Bless and sanctify my soul with heavenly benediction, that it may become thy holy dwelling-place and an abode of thine eternal glory, and may naught be found that can offend the eyes of thy sovereignty in the temple thou deignest to enter. In accordance with the magnitude of thy goodness and the multitude of thy mercies, look on me, and hear the prayer of thy poor servant, exiled afar in the region of death's shadow. Protect and keep the soul of thy little servant amid so many dangers of a life corruptible, and, thy grace accompanying, guide him by a way of peace to the homeland of everlasting brightness. Amen.

BOOK IV

A DEVOUT CALL TO HOLY COMMUNION

BOOK IV

A DEVOUT CALL TO HOLY COMMUNION

The Voice of Christ

COME UNTO me all ye that labour and are heavy laden, and I will refresh you says the Lord. The bread that I will give is my flesh, for the life of the world. Take and eat: this is my body which is given for you: take this in remembrance of me. He who eats my flesh and drinks my blood dwells in me and I in him. The words that I have told you are spirit and life.

1. With what great reverence Christ should be received

VOICE OF the Disciple.

These are thy words, O Christ the Truth eternal, though not spoken at one time, nor written down in one place. So because they are truly thine, they are all to be gratefully and faithfully received by me. They are thine, and thou didst send them forth, and they are mine too because thou didst utter them for my welfare. I take them gladly from thy lips, so that they may be the more deeply set in my heart. They stir me, these words of such tender grace, full of sweetness and love. But my own failings make me afraid of sharing in such mysteries, and an unclean conscience drives me back. The sweetness of thy words invites me, but the multitude of my offences weighs me down. Thou bidst me come trustfully to thee if I would have part with thee, and take the food of life immortal if I would gain eternal life and glory.

Come to me, sayest thou, all ye who labour and are heavy laden, and I will refresh you. O sweet and lovable word to the ear of a sinner, that thou, my Lord God, should invite the poor and destitute into union with thy most holy body.

But who am I O Lord that I should presume to come to thee? Behold the heaven of heavens cannot contain thee, and thou sayest, come all of you to me. What means this most gracious honour, and so lovely an invitation? How shall I dare to come, I who know of nothing good in me on which I may count? How shall I bring thee into my home, I who have so often shocked thy most kindly face? Angels and archangels stand in awe, the saintly and righteous have a reverent fear, and yet thou sayest, come ye all to me.

Unless thou O Lord had said this, who would believe it to be true? And unless thou thyself hadst bidden, who would venture to draw near? See how Noah, a just man, worked a hundred years at making the ark that he with a few might be saved; and how can I in one hour prepare myself to take with reverence the maker of the world? Moses, thy great servant and thy peculiar friend, made an ark of imperishable wood, which he covered with purest gold, in which he could place the tables of the law; and shall I, a perishable creature, dare to receive so lightly thee, the founder of law and giver of life? Solomon, wisest of Israel's kings, was seven years building a magnificent temple to the praise of thy name, and celebrated for the feast of its dedication, offered a thousand peace-offerings, and with resounding trumpet and jubilation, solemnly set the ark of the covenant in the place prepared for it; and how shall I, hapless and poorest of men, bring thee into my house, I that hardly know how to spend half an hour in devotion, and only wish that I could once spend worthily even that half hour?

O my God, how much they strove to please thee! Ah, what a trifle it is that I do; how short a time I spend in preparing myself for communion. Rarely quite calm within;

most seldom clear of every distraction. Yet surely in the presence of saving divinity, no unbecoming thought should intrude, and no created thing take possession; for I am about to welcome as guest, not an angel, but the Lord of angels. Yet how vast is the distance between the ark of the covenant with its dead ashes, and thy most pure body with its unutterable powers; between these legal sacrifices, mere shadowings of things to come, and the actual offering of thy body, the completion of all ancient sacrifices!

Why then do I not burn with more ardent love towards thy sacred presence; why do I not prepare myself with greater care to taste thy holy things; when those old saintly patriarchs and prophets, and kings and princes too with all the people, showed such depth of devotion in divine worship?

David, a truly devout king, danced with all his might before the ark of God, having in mind the good things granted to the fathers of old; he fashioned various kinds of instruments, he produced psalms and taught how to sing them joyously; and filled with the inspiration of the holy Spirit he himself often played on the lute, and taught the people of Israel to praise God with the whole heart, and to bless and proclaim his deeds each day with melodious voice.

If such devotion was accorded at that time before the ark of testimony, and such quickening of praise sprang up, what reverence and devotion should there now be for me and all Christian people in the presence of the sacrament, in taking the sublime body of Christ?

Many run about to various places to see relics of the saints, and are amazed at hearing of their deeds, gaze at the splendid buildings of their shrines, and kiss their sacred bones folded in silk and gold; and lo thou, my God, holy of holies, maker of men and lord of angels, art here present with me on the altar. The inspecting of such things is often mere human curiosity and the novelty of something not seen before, and small fruit of betterment is brought back, especially where there is such frivolous running about with no real change of heart. But here in the sacrament of the altar thou art completely present my God the man Christ Jesus, where too is felt the full enjoyment of everlasting well-being whenever thou art worthily and devoutly received. Assuredly no levity of mind draws one to this, nor curiosity, nor sensuous emotion, but firm faith, devout hope, and genuine love.

O God, invisible founder of the world, how wondrously thou dealest with us, how sweetly and graciously thou sharest with thy chosen ones, to whom thou offerest thyself in the taking of the sacrament. For this surpasses all understanding, this peculiarly draws the hearts of the devout and kindles feeling. For those thy true faithful ones who plan out their whole life towards the better way receive frequently a large gift of devotion and a love of virtue from this most worthy sacrament.

O grace of the sacrament, wonderful and secret, which the trusting ones of Christ know so well, but which the faithless and enslaved to sin cannot experience. In this sacrament spiritual influence is communicated, lost power is restored to the soul, and beauty deformed by sin returns. At times this influence is so great that, through the abounding devotion offered, not only the mind but also the weakened body feels an increased strength given to it.

Hence we should deeply regret and deplore our coldness and indifference through which we are not drawn with intenser affection to receive Christ in whom rests all hope and desert of those to be made whole. For he himself is our means of holiness and release, himself the comfort of wayfarers and eternal fruition of saints. Much should be our sorrow then that many so seldom turn to this wholesome mystery which delights heaven and keeps the whole world from decay.

O the blindness and hardness of the human heart that does not more earnestly heed such an unspeakable gift, but through daily habit falls away into utter disregard. For if in one place only this most holy sacrament were observed, and consecrated on earth by only one priest, with what longing, think you, would men be drawn to that place, and to such a priest of God, in order that they might see the divine mysteries celebrated. But how many priests are made, and Christ is offered in many places, so that the grace and love of God to man appears the greater the more widely the sacred communion is spread throughout the world.

Thanks to thee good Jesu, shepherd everlasting, who deignest to refresh us poor and exiled ones by thy precious body and blood, and even to call us by words from thine own mouth to receive these mysteries, saying, Come unto me all ye who labour and are heavy laden, and I will refresh you.

2. What great goodness and love are shown from God to man in the sacrament

VOICE OF the Disciple.

Relying on thy goodness and great pity, O God, I the sick come to the healer, hungering and thirsting for the fount of life, the destitute to the king of heaven, the servant to the master, the creature to the creator, the desolate one to my kindly comforter. But why should this be mine, that thou shouldst come to me? Who am I that thou shouldst give thyself to me? How should a sinner dare appear before thee, and how canst thou deign to come to a sinner? Thou knowest thy servant, and art aware that he has no good in him that thou shouldst bestow this.

Therefore I confess my worthlessness, I acknowledge thy goodness, I praise thy kindness, and I give thanks for thine excelling love. For thou doest this out of thine own self and not because of my deserving, so that thy goodness may become better known to me, thy love more fully implanted, and humility be more completely made mine. So since this is thy pleasure, and thou hast so ordered it to be, thy kindly thought pleases me too, and I would that my hardness may not be in the way.

O most sweet and kind Jesu, how much reverence and gratitude is due to thee, with perpetual praise, for the sustaining power of thy sacred body, whose worth no man has found the means to unfold? But what shall I meditate as I come in this communion to my Lord whom I cannot worship as I ought, and yet devoutly yearn to receive? What can I ponder on better and with more benefit than humbling myself before thee, and exalting thy goodness infinitely beyond me?

I praise and exalt thee everlastingly, my God, and throw myself upon thee in the depth of my low estate. Lo, thou the saint of saints, and I the meanest of sinners. Lo, thou bendest thyself down to me who am not worthy to look up to thee. Lo, thou comest to me, thou choosest to be with me, thou askest me to thy supper. Thou wilt give me heavenly food, and angels' bread to eat. Nought else indeed than thy very self, the living bread who came down out of heaven and gives the world life.

See whence comes this love, how pity shines through it, what great thanksgivings and praises are thy due for these. O how salutary and helpful was that plan of thine when thou didst institute this; how sweet and joyous the supper when thou gavest thyself as food! O how wonderful that act of thine O Lord; how potent thy goodness; how unfailing thy truth!

For thou didst say the word and all is done; and that which thou hast ordered is accomplished. A thing of wonder and befitting faith, and mastering the human mind: that thou O Lord my God, true God and man, should intimately link thyself with the common form of bread and wine, and be eaten by the partaker without being consumed. Thou Lord of all worlds, who hast need of none, hast chosen to dwell in us through thy sacrament, keep my heart and body unstained; that with clean and happy conscience I may often be able to celebrate and receive for my perpetual welfare thy mysteries which thou didst mainly sanction and institute for thy glory and as an enduring memorial.

Rejoice, my soul, and give thanks to God for so noble a gift and unique a comfort bequeathed to you in this vale of tears. For as often as you renew this mystery and receive Christ's body, so often do you enact the work of your redemption, and are made partaker in all the merits of Christ. For Christ's love never grew less, and the greatness of his self-offering can never be taken away.

Therefore you ought always to settle yourself to this with a freshly renewed mind, and ponder with earnest thought the great mystery of salvation. Thus when you celebrate or hear mass, it should seem to you great, new, and joyous; as if this very day Christ, descending first into the Virgin's womb, was made man; or, hanging on the cross for the saving of men, has suffered and died.

3. How helpful it is to communicate frequently

VOICE OF the Disciple.

Lo, I come to thee O Lord, so that through thy gift it may be well with me, and I be made glad in thy holy feast, as thou O God hast prepared in thy tenderness for the needy. Behold, all that I can or should desire is in thee; thou my health and restoration, hope and endurance, honour and glory.

Therefore make the soul of thy servant rejoice this day, since I lift up my soul to thee Lord Jesu. I long to receive thee now devoutly and reverently; I yearn to bring thee into my dwelling, that with Zaccheus I may become worthy of being blessed by thee, and be counted among the sons of

Abraham. My soul burns for thy body; my heart longs to be one with thee. Give me thyself and it suffices, for no comfort counts compared with thee.

I cannot live without thee, and without thy coming I cannot exist. And so I need to come frequently to thee to receive again the medicine of my well-being, lest it chance I lose hope on the way if deprived of celestial food. For so, most pitying Jesus, thou once in preaching to the throng and healing varied diseases didst say: I will not send them home fasting lest they faint on the way.

Therefore deal in the same way with me, thou who hast left thyself in the sacrament for the comfort of the faithful. For thou art the sweet restorer of the soul, and he who worthily absorbs thee will be partaker and heir of eternal glory. To me who so often err and sin, so quickly slacken and give way, it is specially necessary that by frequent prayers and confessions, and the receiving of thy sacred body, I should renew, purify, and enkindle myself, lest haply by keeping away too long I should lose the will for holiness. For a man's senses incline towards evil from his youth, and unless a divine remedy helps him he slips into worse ways.

Holy Communion, therefore, draws him back from evil, and strengthens him for good. For if now I am so often careless and half-hearted when I communicate or celebrate, what would happen if I did not take this remedy nor seek so mighty a help? And though I may not be prepared or in the right mood to celebrate every day, yet at suitable times I will try to realise the divine mysteries, and make myself a sharer in so great a favour. For this is the one chief comfort of the trusting soul as long as it journeys in mortal flesh apart from thee, that the more often it thinks of its God it receives its beloved with a devout mind.

Oh, the wondrous condescending of thy kindness towards us, that thou O Lord God, creator and life-giver of all spirits, deignest to come to a poor little soul and with thy complete divinity and humanity to satisfy his eager want. O happy mind and blessed soul, privileged to receive thee its Lord God in devotion, and in receiving thee to be filled with spiritual gladness. O how great a master it receives, how beloved a guest it leads in, how joyous a companion it takes to itself, how faithful a friend it welcomes, how fair and noble a bridegroom it embraces, to be loved before all loves, and beyond all possible desires.

My most sweet beloved, may heaven and earth and all their array be hushed before thy face, for whatever worth and loveliness they possess are of thy kindly giving and can never rise to the beauty of thy name whose wisdom is measureless.

4. That many blessings are given to those who communicate devoutly

VOICE OF the Disciple.

O Lord my God, go before the servant with blessings of tenderness, so that I may be made fit to approach the glorious sacrament worthily and devoutly. Awake my heart to thee, and free me from heavy listlessness. Come to me with thy liberating power that in spirit I may taste thy sweetness, which lies completely hidden in this sacrament as in a fountain. Give light also to my eyes to gaze into so deep a mystery, and strengthen me to believe it with undoubting faith. For it is thy doing, no human power; thy sacred institution, no invention of man. For no-one can of himself grasp and understand those things which transcend even the subtlety of angels.

What then can I, an unworthy sinner, dust and ashes, search out and retain concerning so lofty a secret? O Lord, I come to thee with hope and awe, with the singleness of my heart, with good firm trust, and at thy command, and truly believe that thou art here present in the sacrament, God and man. Thou wishest me to receive thee and unite my very self to thee in love.

Wherefore I beseech thy pity, and implore special grace to be given me for this, so that I may utterly dissolve in thee, and overflow with love, and no more allow any alien comfort. For this most high and honoured sacrament is the health of soul and body, the medicine for all spiritual faintness by which my faults are cured, passions bridled, temptations overcome or weakened, larger grace instilled, virtue begun is made to grow, faith steadied, hope strengthened, and love set afire and enlarged.

For thou hast freely given and still often givest many blessings through the sacrament to thy beloved who devoutly communicate, O my God, sustainer of my soul, restorer of human frailty, and giver of every inward consolation. For thou pervadest them with many a solace against varied trouble, and dost lift them out of the depths of dejection into hope of thy protection, and with some new favour dost revive and enlighten them inwardly, so that those who at first felt themselves uneasy and wanting, being afterwards refreshed with heavenly food and drink, find themselves altered for the better.

In such a way thou dealest with thy chosen that they may truly know and openly test how great is their own weakness and what goodness and favour they gain from thee, since in themselves they are cold, hard and undevout, through thee they are enabled to become fervent, keen and devout. For who can with humility draw near the fount of sweetness and not bring away from it some little of that sweetness? Or who can stand near a well-filled fire and not receive some little heat from it? And thou art a fountain always full and overflowing, a fire always burning and never dying down.

So, though I may not draw from the fountain's own fulness, nor even drink my fill, yet will I set my mouth to the opening of this celestial conduit, that I may take from it a tiny drop to refresh my thirst, and not stay utterly parched. And if as yet I cannot be truly heaven-like, and burn like cherubim and seraphim, yet I will try to set myself towards devotion, and to make my heart ready, so that I may acquire even a tiny flame of divine fire through humbly partaking of the life-giving sacrament. But whatever I lack, O good Jesu, most holy saviour, kindly and graciously supply thou for me; thou who didst deign to call every one to thee, saying,—Come unto me all ye that labour and are heavy-laden, and I will refresh you.

I indeed toil in the sweat of my brow, am torn with sorrow of heart, laden with sins, made restless with temptations, entangled and oppressed with many evil passions, and there is none to help, none to free and make me whole, but thou, O Lord God, my Saviour, to whom I yield myself and all that is mine, for thee to guard and lead on to the life eternal. For the praise and glory of thy name, receive me; thou who hast prepared thy body and blood for my food and drink.

Be near, O Lord my saving God, that in frequenting thy mystery the fervour of my devotion may increase.

5. Of the dignity of the sacrament and of a priest's part

VOICE OF the Beloved.

If you had angelic purity and the holiness of saint John Baptist you would not of yourself be worthy of receiving or handling this sacrament. For it is not due to human merits that a man should consecrate and administer Christ's sacrament and receive as food the bread of angels. Sublime is the ministry, and great the dignity of priests to whom is given what is not granted to angels. For priests alone, rightly ordained in the church, have power to celebrate and consecrate Christ's body.

The priest is indeed the servant of God, using God's word at God's bidding and institution; but God is the prime author there, and the invisible worker, to whom all is subject as he wills, all obey as he commands. In this most excellent sacrament therefore you should trust the all-powerful God more than your own opinion or any visible sign. And for the same reason you must come to this act with fear and reverence.

Look to yourself, and see whose is the ministry that was entrusted to you by the laying on of the bishop's hand. See, you are made a priest, and consecrated in order to celebrate. Look now that you offer the sacrifice to God faithfully and devoutly at the proper time, and present yourself blameless. You have not lightened your burden, but are now bound with a stricter cord of discipline, and held to a greater perfection of holiness.

A priest should be adorned with all the virtues, and show an example of good life to others. His walk in life should not be with the popular and common ways of men, but with angels in heaven and with perfect men on earth. A priest clad in sacred vestments acts in Christ's stead when, with entreaty and humility, he prays to God for himself and for all the people. Before and behind him he has the sign of the master's cross, as a continual reminder of Christ's passion. He carries the cross before on the chasuble that he may carefully note the footsteps of Christ and fervently strive to follow. He is sealed with the cross behind him that for God he may bear forgivingly whatever crosses are laid upon him by others. He bears the cross before him that he may lament his own sins; behind him that in pity he may also mourn the transgressions of others, and realise that he is placed midway between God and the sinner; nor may he slacken in prayer and the holy offering till he has succeeded in winning grace and pity.

Whenever a priest celebrates he gives honour to God, delights angels, builds up the church, helps the living, assures rest to the dead, and makes himself partaker of all good things.

6. The question of preparing for communion

VOICE OF the Disciple.

When I compare thy greatness, Lord, and my worthlessness, I am exceedingly shaken and inwardly confused. For if I do not come near, I am missing life; and if I thrust myself in, I risk offending. So what shall I do, my God, my helper and adviser in times of need? Teach thou me the right way, set some brief exercise suitable to the holy communion. For it is right to learn how I ought indeed to prepare my heart devoutly and reverently for thee, in order to receive thy sacrament for my well-being, or again for the celebrating of so great and divine a sacrifice.

7. Of examining one's own conscience and planning amendment

VOICE OF the Beloved.

Above everything a priest of God should come to this sacrament to celebrate, touch and partake with deep humility of heart and reverent prayer, 'with full faith and a duteous intent on God's honour. Examine your conscience diligently and, as far as you can, make it clean and bright by true contrition and lowly confession, so that you may have nothing to weigh you down, or know of anything to cause you remorse and hinder your ready access. Feel true displeasure at all your sins as a whole, and sorrow and sigh more particularly over your daily transgressions. And if time allows, confess in the heart's secrecy all the unhappiness of your sufferings.

Bemoan and grieve that you are still so carnal and wordly, so alive to passions, so filled with impulses of lust, so unguarded in the outward senses, so often entangled with many empty fantasies, so much inclined to external things, so indifferent to those within, so ready for laughter and licence, so hardened towards tears and compunction, so quick for ease and bodily comforts, so slow to rigour and zeal, so eager to hear about news and see things of beauty, so remiss to draw in the lowly and downcast, so covetous to possess much, so close in giving away, so tenacious in keeping, so thoughtless in speech, so uncontrolled in keeping silence, so ill-ordered in manners, so rude in actions, so unrestrained about food, so deaf to God's word, so quick to rest, so slow to work, so wakeful to idle tales, so drowsy at holy vigils, so hasty for their end, so drifting in attention, so careless in saying the Hours, so tepid in celebrating, so dry in communicating, so quickly distracted, so seldom fully self-collected, so suddenly stirred to anger, so easily offended by another, so apt to judge, so sharp in censure, so joyous in prosperity, so weak in adversity, so often making many good intentions, and carrying them into little effect.

For these and other failings of yours, acknowledged and deplored with sorrow and great dissatisfaction at your own frailty, set down a firm resolve to be continually amending your life, and pressing on to better ways. Then, with complete resignation and unimpaired will, offer yourself on the altar of your heart a continuous burnt offering in honour of my name; that is, loyally entrusting your body and soul to me, and so, to that extent, become worthy to draw near and offer a sacrifice to God, and to receive the sacrament of my body for your good.

For there is no worthier offering nor greater reparation for cleaning faults away than to offer oneself purely and entirely to God with the oblation of Christ's body in the Mass and in the Communion. If a man does what he can, and truly repents, so often as ever he comes to me for pardon and favour, I who live, says the Lord, wish not the sinner's death, but rather that he turn and live, for I will no longer keep the memory of his sins, but all shall be forgiven him.

8. Of Christ's offering on the cross and our own self-surrender

VOICE OF the Beloved.

As I freely offered myself to God the Father for your sins, with my hands stretched on the cross and body stripped, so that nothing was left in me which might be changed into a sacrifice of divine appeasing, so should you willingly offer yourself to me daily in the Mass as a clean and holy oblation with all your might and affection as profoundly as you can.

What more do I ask of you than that you strive to yield yourself to me absolutely? I care nothing for whatever else you give except yourself, because I seek not your gift but you. Just as it would not satisfy you to possess all but me, so neither can it please me whatever you give without offering yourself. Offer up yourself to me, and give self wholly for God, and the offering will be accepted. Lo, I offered myself entirely to the Father for you; I gave too my body and blood as food, that I might be wholly yours, and you lastingly mine. But if you take your stand on self, without freely offering up your own to my will, it is no complete oblation, nor will there be perfect union between us.

Therefore a spontaneous offering of yourself into the hands of God should precede all your acts if you wish to attain to freedom and grace. This is why so few are made shining lights and inwardly free, because they do not know how to deny themselves entirely. That sentence of mine stands fast, unless a man gives up in everything he cannot be my disciple. Therefore if you would be a disciple offer yourself to me with all you care for.

9. *That we ought to offer ourselves and all that is ours to God, and pray for all*

VOICE OF the Disciple.

O Lord, all things in heaven and earth are thine. I would offer myself to thee in free surrender, to remain for ever thine. O Lord, in singleness of my heart I lay myself before thee this day, a servant for ever in obedience and with the offering of perpetual praise. Receive me together with this holy oblation of thy precious body which I offer to thee this day in the presence of angels who stand invisibly by, that it may be for the saving of me and of all thy people.

Lord on thine altar of conciliation I offer thee all my sins and faults that I have committed before thee and thy holy angels from the day when first capable of sin up to this hour, that thou mayst burn them all alike and consume them in the fire of thy love, and take out all the stains of my sin, and cleanse my conscience of every wrong, and restore to me thy grace which I lost by sin, forgiving everything completely, and mercifully drawing me to thee with a kiss of peace.

What can I do about my sins but humbly confess and lament them, and unceasingly beseech thy favour? I entreat thee to hear me favourably, when I stand before thee, my God. All my sins are most displeasing to me; I never wish to commit them again, but grieve over them and will grieve as long as I live, ready to do penance and to make satisfaction to the utmost.

Forgive me, O God, forgive me my sins, through thy holy name; let it be well with my soul which thou hast redeemed by thy precious blood. See, I place myself at thy mercy, I yield myself into thy hands; deal with me in the spirit of thy goodness, not according to my evil and unrighteous way.

I offer to thee as well all good of mine however poor and imperfect, for thee to amend and sanctify, so that it become welcome and acceptable to thee, and be evermore drawn on to better things, and bring me, an indolent and useless mannikin, to a blessed and praiseworthy end.

I also offer to thee every pious longing of devout souls, the needs of parents, friends, brothers, sisters, and all my dear ones, and of those who for love of thee have done good to me or to others, and who have wished and begged me to say prayers and masses for them and all theirs, whether they still live in the flesh or are dead to the world; that all may feel the dawning help of thy grace, the effect of consolation, protection from dangers, freedom from pains, and that, delivered from all evils, they may joyfully pay thee abounding thanks.

I offer also to thee prayers and sacrifices of intercession, especially for those who in any way have hurt, saddened, or spoken ill of me, or caused me any loss or grievance; and for all those I may at any time have annoyed, troubled, burdened and scandalised by words or deeds, knowingly or in ignorance, that thou mayst forgive us all alike our own sins and our offences against each other.

Take away from our hearts, O Lord, all suspicion, resentment, anger and contention, and whatever can injure charity and lessen brotherly love. Pity, pity, Lord, those who ask thy mercy; give favour to the needy, and make us so to live that we may be worthy to enjoy thy grace and press on to life eternal, Amen.

10. That holy communion is not to be lightly put aside

VOICE OF the Beloved.

You must frequently return to the source of grace and divine mercy, to the fount of goodness and perfect purity, so that you may be cured of your passions and sins, and be made stronger and more watchful against the temptations and wiles of the devil. The enemy, knowing the very great gain and healing that lies in holy communion, strives his hardest by every method and opportunity to hinder and keep back the faithful and devout. So that some in making themselves ready for holy communion suffer worse than ever from Satan's suggestions.

For the evil spirit, as it is written in Job, comes among the sons of God to trouble them with his usual villainy, either to make them excessively cautious and perplexed, so that he may lessen their emotions, or, by attacking, may undermine their faith, so that possibly they may either give up the communion entirely or approach it tepidly. But one must not trouble in the least about his subtleties and delusions, however foul and frightening, for all such phantasms must be made to recoil upon his own head. The wretch is to be scorned and derided, and holy communion is not to be put aside because of his taunts or the disquiets he rouses.

Then again, an over-eager longing to feel devotion, and an excessive anxiety as to making confession, often become a hindrance. Do as the wise advise, and put aside anxiety and scruple, for these impede God's grace and destroy the mind's devoutness. Do not put off holy communion for any little qualm or trouble, but go the speedier to confess it, and freely forgive all injuries done to you by others. Certainly if you have hurt anyone, humbly ask forgiveness, and God will freely pardon you.

What good is it to put off confession for a long time, or to defer holy communion? Cleanse yourself first of all, spit out the poison quickly, make haste to take the medicine, and you will feel better than if you had made a long delay. If you put it aside today for one thing, perhaps tomorrow something else more important will arise, and so you may be kept from communion a long while and become still more unready. As quickly as possible shake yourself free from current depression and inaction, for it does no good to linger in hesitation, to go on long with an unsettled mind, and to cut oneself off from divine things for the sake of every-day obstacles. It is indeed most harmful to put off communion for long because it usually leads to grave apathy.

Alas, some tepid and careless ones happily welcome any hindrances to confession, and simply want to defer holy communion lest they should feel bound to keep a stricter guard over themselves. Oh what little love and what feeble devotion they have who so easily postpone holy communion. How happy and acceptable to God is he who so lives and safeguards his conscience with such purity that he is ready and strongly moved to communicate every day if he might, and could do so without observation.

If anyone abstains at times through humility, or because of some legitimate hindrance, he is to be commended for reverence. But if apathy should creep over him, he must rouse himself and do his best, and the Lord will help his desire of a good intention, that which he specially looks for. But when he is honestly prevented he will always keep a good will and a pious intention of communicating, and so will not miss the fruit of the sacrament. For every day and every hour any devout soul can beneficially and unprevented attain to spiritual communion with Christ, yet still on certain days and at a stated time he ought to receive sacramentally, with loving reverence, the body of his Redeemer, and keep in view God's honour and praise rather than his own consolation.

For he communicates mystically and is invisibly refreshed as often as he devoutly reflects on the mystery of Christ's incarnation and suffering, and is inflamed with love of him. On the other hand he who does not prepare himself unless a festival is near or mere habit drives him will often be unprepared.

Blessed is he who offers self as a burnt offering to the Lord whenever he celebrates or communicates. Be not too leisurely nor hurried in celebrating, but keep to the good ordinary method of those with whom you live. You ought not to cause irritation and weariness to others, but keep the usual way according to the practice of your fathers, and consider more what helps others than what serves your own devotion and feeling.

11. That Christ's body and the holy scriptures are most needful to the faithful soul

VOICE OF the Disciple.

O most sweet Lord Jesus, how great is the delight of a devout soul sharing in the feast, where there is no other food placed for him to eat but thyself, his one beloved, longed for beyond all his heart's desires. Surely for me indeed it would be sweet to shed tears of deepest feeling in thy presence, and with grateful Magdalen wash thy feet with tears. But where is this devotion, where the full flow of consecrated tears? Assuredly in beholding thee and thy holy angels my whole heart should burn and weep for joy. For I have thee verily present in the sacrament though concealed in a different form. For my eyes could not endure to see thee in thine own divine brightness, nor could the whole world stand up to the splendour of thy kingly glory.

So in this thou takest note of my helplessness,—that thou veilest thyself under a sacrament. Truly I possess and adore him whom angels in heaven worship; but I still for a while in faith, they in vision and without a veil. I must be satisfied with the light of true faith, and walk in it till the day of eternal shining rises, and the shadow of forms decline. But when that which is perfect comes the need of sacraments will cease, for those blest with heavenly glory will need no sacramental healing, for they unceasingly rejoice in God's presence, seeing his glory face to face, and, transformed from brightness to brightness of unfathomable Deity, they

taste the word of God made flesh as it was from the beginning and remains eternally. The thought of these
marvels makes even any kind of spiritual comfort a heavy
weariness to me because so long as I do not see my Lord
clearly in his glory I take all that I see or hear in the world
as naught.

Thou O God art my witness that nothing can comfort me,
nothing made can give me rest, but thou my God whom I
long to contemplate eternally. But this is impossible whilst
I am held in this mortal state, therefore I must fashion myself
to perfect patience, and submit myself in every wish to thee.
For thy saints too, O Lord, who now rejoice with thee in
the kingdom of heaven, whilst they lived waited in faith and
great patience for the coming of thy glory. What they
believed, I believe; what they hoped for, I hope for; where
they have attained, I by thy grace trust to come. Meantime
I will walk in faith, strengthened by the examples of the
saints; I too will use holy books for solace and for a mirror
of life; and, beyond all these, thy most holy body for sole
remedy and refuge.

For I feel that two things are most essential for me in this
life, without which this hapless life would be unbearable to
me. Confined in the prison of this body I know myself in
need of two things, namely food and light. Therefore to me
the weakling thou didst give thy holy body for the refreshing of mind and body, and hast placed thy word as a
lamp for my feet. Without these two I could not live
aright, for God's word is the light of my soul, and thy
sacrament the bread of life. These can also be called the two
tables set this side and that in the treasury of holy church.
One table is that of the sacred altar having holy bread
that is Christ's precious body; the other is that of divine
law containing holy teaching, instructing right faith, and
leading steadily onward to the inner veil where is the holy
of holies.

Thanks be to thee, O Lord Jesus, light of eternal light,

for the table of holy doctrine which thou hast supplied for us by thy ministers, apostles, prophets and other teachers. Thanks be to thee, Creator and Redeemer of men, who, to show thy love to the whole world, hast prepared a great supper in which thou hast set before us to be eaten, not a figurative lamb, but thy most holy body and blood, making all the faithful joyous in a sacred banquet, and filling them with the chalice of salvation in which are all the delights of paradise, and they, the holy angels, feast with us though with a happier sweetness.

O how great and honourable is the office of priests to whom is given to consecrate with sacred words the Lord of glory: with their lips to bless, with their hands to hold, with their own mouth to receive, and to administer to others. O how clean should be the hands, how pure the mouth, how holy the body, how spotless the heart of a priest, to whom there enters so often the author of purity. Out of the mouth of a priest who so often received the sacrament of Christ should come nothing but the holy, nothing but the upright and helpful. Simple and modest should be his eyes which are accustomed to look upon the body of Christ. Pure and lifted heavenward the hands that are used to touch tne Creator of heaven and earth. In the law it was to the priests especially said: Be thou holy, for I the Lord thy God am holy.

Almighty God help us by thy grace that we who have undertaken the priestly office may be able to serve thee worthily and devoutly in utmost purity and sound conscience. And if we be unable to live in such innocence as we ought, yet grant us duly to mourn the wrongs we have done, and in a spirit of humility, and with settled purpose of good will, to serve thee more fervently for the rest of our days.

12. *That he who would take communion should prepare himself for Christ with great care*

VOICE OF the Beloved.

I am the lover of purity, and the giver of all holiness. I look for the pure heart, and there is my place of rest. Prepare for me a goodly furnished room, and I and my disciples will keep a paschal feast with you. If you would have me come to you and stay with you, purge out old ferment, and clean the dwelling-place of your heart. Shut out all that is earthly, and all the din of vices; sit like a sparrow alone on a roof, and think over thy wrong-doings in the bitterness of thy soul. For every lover prepares for his beloved the best and most beautiful place, because by this is seen the affection borne towards the loved one. Yet understand that by no worth of your own doing can you make sufficient preparation, even if you prepared yourself for a whole year, keeping nothing else in mind. But only out of my goodness and grace are you allowed to come to my table; it is as if a beggar had been asked to a rich man's dinner, and had nothing else to give him in return for his kindness except to carry himself humbly and give him repeated thanks.

Do what lies in you and do it deliberately, not out of habit, nor from compulsion, but with fear and reverence and affection receive the body of thy beloved Lord God deigning to come to you. It is I who called, I wished it to be done; I will fill up what is lacking in you; come and receive me.

When I impart the grace of devotion, give thanks to your God, not because you deserved it but because I pitied you. If you have no such grace but feel yourself rather to be dry, persevere in prayer, sigh and knock; and cease not until you are made fit to receive a crumb or a drop of saving grace. You need me; I do not need you. Nor do you come to make me holy, but I come to make you holy and better. You come that you may be sanctified by me and made one with me; that you may receive new power and be kindled afresh to amendment. Do not neglect this grace, but prepare your heart with every care, and draw in your beloved to you.

Yet you must not only prepare yourself for devotion before communion, but also keep yourself earnestly in it after receiving the sacrament. Vigilance is no less required afterwards than devout preparation before. For careful watch afterwards is the best preparation for getting more grace another time. If one is too eager for helps from without he will find himself all the more unready. Beware of talking much, live a hidden life and enjoy your God, for you hold him whom all the world cannot take from you. I am he to whom you should wholly yield yourself, so that you no longer live in yourself but in me, with all anxiety gone.

13. That the devout soul should whole-heartedly aim at union with Christ in the sacrament

VOICE OF the Disciple.

Who, Lord, will make it my very own to find thee and open all my heart to thee, and enjoy thee as my soul desires, while none may despise me, nor any created thing disturb me, but thou alone speak to me and I to thee, as a lover is wont to speak to a loved one and friend to feast with friend? This I pray for, this I desire, that I may become entirely one with thee, and my heart be drawn away from all created things, and I learn yet more through holy communion and frequent celebration to taste the heavenly and eternal realities.

Ah Lord God, when shall I be wholly united with and lost in thee, my self completely forgotten? Thou in me and I in thee, and so in one let us remain together. Truly thou art my beloved, the chosen out of thousands, in whom my soul delights to dwell all the days of her life. Thou truly art my bringer of peace with whom is highest peace and true rest, without whom all is toil and sorrow and infinite misery. Truly thou art the God who hides himself, and thy wisdom dwells not among the wicked, but thy converse is with the lowly and simple.

O how gentle is thy spirit, O Lord, who to show thy tenderness to thy sons deignest to refresh them with the sweetest of bread coming down from heaven. Truly there is no other nation so great as to have God as near to them as thou our God art near to all thy faithful ones, to whom, for daily comfort and up-lifting of the heart to heaven, thou givest thyself to be eaten and enjoyed. For what other race is so illustrious as the Christian people, or what creature under heaven so loved as the devout soul to whom God enters in to feed it with his glorious flesh.

O wordless grace; O wondrous condescension, O measureless love, uniquely spent on man. But what shall I give back to the Lord for this favour, for love so excelling? There is nothing I can give more acceptable than to offer up my heart wholly to God and be most closely united to him. Then shall all within me rejoice when my soul shall be perfectly one with God. Then will he say to me: If you long to be with me, I will be with you. And I will answer him: Deign, Lord, to abide with me; I will gladly stay with thee; this is my whole desire, that my heart be made one with thee.

14. Of the ardent longing of certain devout ones for Christ's body

VOICE OF the Disciple.

O how great the store of thy sweetness, Lord, which thou hast hidden up for those who revere thee. When I recall certain devout souls who come to thy sacrament, Lord, with the greatest devotion and feeling, then am I often disconcerted as to myself, and blush with shame that so languidly and coldly I approach thine altar and the table of holy communion; that I remain so arid and unmoved at heart; that I am not totally inflamed before thee my God, nor so fervently drawn to thee and affected as many of the devout were, who from excessive desire of communion and heartfelt love could not hold back their tears, but with utterance of heart and body alike panted from their inmost being for thee, O God, the living fountain, unable in any other way to temper or satisfy their hunger except by receiving thy body with all joy and spiritual eagerness. O their true and burning faith that seems a proving witness to thy sacred presence! For they truly recognise their Lord in the breaking of bread as their heart so strongly burns in them through Jesus walking with them. Such affection and devotion, such impetuous love and ardour, are often far from me.

Take pity on me, kind Jesus, gentle and gracious, and let thy poor mendicant feel sometimes at least a little of that heartfelt love of thee in the holy communion; so that my faith may be more strengthened, hope in thy goodness increased, and love once perfectly kindled and the heavenly manna tasted they may never fail. And yet thy mercy can give me even the longed-for grace, and visit me most benignly with spiritual fervour in the day when it pleases thee to come. For though I do not burn with such a yearning as thy specially devout ones, yet through thy favour I have a longing for that great flaming desire, wishing and praying that I may be made a sharer with all such fervid lovers of thine and be reckoned in their holy company.

15. That the gift of devotion is to be gained by humility and self-denial

Voice of the Beloved.

You should eagerly seek the grace of devoutness, ask it with longing, look for it patiently and with confidence, accept it with thankfulness, preserve it humbly, take pains to work with it, and leave to God the extent and way of the heavenly visitation till it comes. You should particularly be humble about yourself when you feel little or no inward devoutness; but not be too cast down nor inordinately depressed. God often gives in one brief instant what for a long time he withheld. Sometimes he gives at last what at the beginning of prayer he delayed giving. If grace were always quickly given, and came for the asking, feeble man could not easily keep it up. For that reason the gift of devotion is to be waited for with good hope and lowly patience.

Yet, when it is not given or when it is mysteriously taken away, impute it to yourself and to your sins. Sometimes it is a very slight thing that hinders or hides grace, if indeed that can be called little and not rather great which holds back such a good. But if you put aside this same small or vast thing, and thoroughly over-ride it, you will get what you ask. For immediately you yield yourself to God, not seeking this nor that for your own pleasure or will, but reposing yourself entirely in him, you will find yourself at one and at peace, for then nothing will taste and please so well as the good pleasure of the divine will.

Whoever will therefore with singleness of heart lift up his intention to God, and empty himself of all disordered love, or dislike of any creature, he will be fitted to receive grace, and worthy of the gift of devoutness. For the Lord gives his blessing there where he finds the vessels empty. And the more thoroughly one renounces the lower things, and the more he dies to self by contempt of self, so much the swifter comes grace, the more abundantly it enters, and the higher it uplifts the freed heart.

Then shall he see and overflow, and his heart shall wonder and be enlarged within him because the Lord's hand is with him, and he has placed himself entirely in his hand, even for ever. Lo, thus shall a man be blessed who with his whole heart seeks God, and has not lifted up his soul towards the unreal, this man in receiving the holy eucharist wins the great favour of divine union because he looks not to his own prayer and comfort, but, beyond all devotion and consolation, to the glory and honour of God.

16. *That we ought to lay our needs open to Christ and ask his help*

Voice of the Disciple.

O most tender and loving Lord whom I now devoutly long to receive; thou knowest my weakness and need, and what I suffer; amid what evils and vices I am cast; how often I am depressed, tempted, confused, and brought low. I come to thee for healing, I pray thee for comfort and support. I speak to one knowing all, to whom all my inmost thoughts are plain, and who alone can perfectly comfort and help me. Thou knowest the good things I need before all else, and how poor I am in the strong qualities.

See how I stand before thee poor and bare, asking favour and imploring compassion. Refresh thy hungering suppliant, melt my coldness in the fire of thy love, illumine my blindness by the brightness of thy presence. Turn all the earthly into bitterness for me, all burdens and crosses into patience, all that is base and time-born into scorn and oblivion. Lift my heart up to thee in heaven, and send me not roaming about the earth. Be thou alone my sweet delight from this present even for evermore, for thou alone art my food and drink, my love and my joy, my dear and all my good.

Oh that by thy presence thou wouldst wholly burn through me, consume and transmute me into thyself, that I might become one spirit with thee by the power of inward union, and the melting of a burning love. Let me not go from thee spiritless and parched, but deal mercifully with me as thou hast often wonderfully done with thy holy ones.

What wonder if I should be completely aflame through thee, and my very self perish, when thou art a fire for ever burning and never dying down, a love purifying the heart and illumining the mind.

17. Of the ardent love and keen desire to receive Christ

Voice of the Disciple.

With deep devotion and burning love, with all the feeling and fervour of the heart, I long to receive thee O Lord, just as many saints and devout souls have yearned for thee in the act of communion, they who were most pleasing to thee by sanctity of life, and were most ardent in devoutness.

O my God, love eternal, my whole good, happiness unending, I receive thee with the keenest desire and the most befitting reverence that any of the saints ever had or could feel. And although I am unworthy to have all those feelings of devotion, yet I offer up to thee my heart's entire affection, as if I alone had all those most delightful ardent longings. Yes, and whatever a pious mind can think of and wish, these with deepest reverence and inmost readiness I bring and offer up to thee. I would keep back nothing for myself, but willingly and most happily sacrifice myself and all that is mine to thee.

O Lord my God, my creator and my redeemer, I would this day receive thee with such feeling, reverence, praise and honour, hope and purity as thy most holy mother the glorious Virgin Mary longed for and received when, to the angel announcing to her the mystery of incarnation, she humbly and devoutly answered: behold the handmaid of the Lord, be it unto me according to thy word. And as thy blessed forerunner, most excellent of saints, John Baptist, rejoicing in thy presence, leaped with the joy of the holy Spirit whilst he was still enclosed in his mother's womb;

and afterwards seeing Jesus walking among men very greatly humbling himself said,—the bridegroom's friend who stands by and listens rejoices with gladness because of the bridegroom's voice; and so would I be enflamed with great and holy desires, and present myself whole-heartedly to thee.

So I offer and render to thee the rejoicings of all devout hearts, the fervent emotions, the mental raptures, the supernatural illuminings, and the celestial visions, together with all the virtues and praises rising and still to rise from every creature in heaven and earth, for me and for all commended to me in prayer, that thou mayst be worthily praised by all and perpetually glorified.

Accept my vows, O Lord my God, and the desires to give unending praise and measureless blessing which are rightly due to thee for thy manifold and unspeakable greatness. These do I offer up and long to offer each day and moment of time, and I beg and entreat all heavenly spirits and the whole of thy faithful ones with prayers and sympathy to render with me thanksgiving and praises.

Let all peoples, tribes, and tongues praise thee, and magnify thy holy and honey-sweet name with highest jubilation and glowing devotion. And may they who reverently and devoutly celebrate thy most high sacrament and receive with full faith be held worthy of finding favour and mercy with thee, and may they humbly pray for me a sinner. And after they have won the wished-for devoutness and tasted the joy of union, and have withdrawn from the celestial holy table very comforted and wondrously refreshed, may they deign to remember poor me.

18. That a man should not be a curious investigator of the sacrament, but a lowly imitator of Christ, submitting his reason to holy faith

VOICE OF the Beloved.

You must beware of curious and useless searching into this most profound sacrament if you would not be plunged into the deeps of doubt. He who is a scrutineer of majesty will be overwhelmed by its glory. God can do more than man can understand. An honest and lowly search into truth is permissible to one always ready to be taught, and striving to walk by the sane precepts of the fathers. Blessed is the simplicity which leaves the difficult paths of questionings, and treads the plain and firm road of God's commands. Many have lost the devout spirit by wishing to pierce through deep things. Faith is demanded of you, and a simple life; not intellectual height nor deep knowledge of God's mysteries. If you do not understand nor grasp things below you how will you lay hold of those above you? Submit to God, and humble your reason to faith, and such light of knowledge will be given you as will be good and needful.

Some are seriously tested as to faith and sacrament yet this is not to be put down to them but rather to the enemy. Never mind. Do not argue with your thoughts, nor answer doubts incited by the devil, but rely on God's words, trust his saints and prophets, and the wicked enemy will fly from you. It often does God's servant much good to bear up against such attacks. For he does not tempt the faithless and the sinners whom he already safely holds; but he tests and harasses the faithful, the devout, in various ways.

Press on therefore with simple and undoubting faith, and come to the sacrament with the reverence of a suppliant, and what you cannot understand entrust safely to God the almighty. God does not mislead you; he is deceived who trusts too much to himself. God walks with the simple, reveals himself to the lowly, gives understanding to the little ones, opens the meaning to pure minds, and hides grace from the inquisitive and conceited.

Human reason is weak and can be misled; but true faith cannot be deceived. All reason and natural research should follow faith, not go before it nor encroach upon it. For faith and love most excel here in this most holy and sublime sacrament, and work in hidden ways. God eternal and boundless and of infinite power does great and unsearchable things in heaven and on earth, and there is no searching out of his marvellous doings. If the works of God were such as to be easily comprehended by human reason they could not be called wonderful or too great for words.